Love Poems

Compiled by Fiona Mackenzie Moore

HarperCollins*Publishers*
Westerhill Road, Bishopbriggs, Glasgow G64 2QT

www.collins.co.uk

First published 2004

Foreword © U. A. Fanthorpe 2004

This compilation © HarperCollins*Publishers* 2004

Reprint 10 9 8 7 6 5 4 3 2 1 0

ISBN 0-00-717781-x

Typeset by Davidson Pre-Press Graphics Ltd, Glasgow

Printed in Italy by Amadeus S.p.a.

CONTENTS

FOREWORD

War, death, landscape, cats, food – all these are worthy of being anthologised, and so they have been. But love comes first. What is it about love?

For one thing, it has many voices. Its poets can be funny or tragic or angry or erotic. There's an infinite range of perspectives: an anthology of love poems is far from monotonous. It can modulate from friendship, through lifelong devotion, to sheer blunt lust. There is He and She, of course, but there is also the reader-over-their-shoulder. Love poems, I suspect, are not just written for that impossible she, but for this expected voyeur. And the interesting thing is that we, the readers, are prepared to take what the poets say, whatever it may be, as gospel truth. This is where love poetry differs from all other kinds.

Fiona Moore's choice can hardly avoid the great and the well-known: we shouldn't think much of an anthology that left out Marvell and Shakespeare, Donne and Betjeman. It's easy for such an anthology to concentrate on the politer end of the spectrum.

But this one embraces the bluntness of Adrian
Mitchell's 'Celia, Celia'

> When I am sad and weary
> When I think all hope has gone
> When I walk along High Holborn
> I think of you with nothing on.

and Lady Mary Wortley Montagu's sound advice
to the bereaved Delia, to 'choose among the pretty
fellows' – in other words, to pursue life, not death.
It gives a very fair share to women (Charlotte Mew
comes out particularly well), and it is generous in
its inclusion of all the periods since love poetry in
the English language began in the time of Anon.
Characteristically, weather figures largely in the early
poems – in fact I might suggest to Moore that her
next anthology might be of weather. But in the
meanwhile, read this for its wit, its generosity, its
bird-song, its consistency. Love and poetry – two
things we're good at.

U. A. Fanthorpe

INTRODUCTION

It little profits (till now) that an idle pupil should make off with *The English Parnassus*. I still have it, and I would like to thank Portree High School English Department for encouraging an early love of poetry which has been rekindled during my research for this book.

I am indebted to U. A. Fanthorpe for her kind foreword and flattered that she thinks I should contemplate another anthology. While I had not particularly noted the weather theme, I hope my selection contains enough elements to ensure there is something for everyone: from the fiery passion of youth to the contented embers of long-established affection; from icy betrayal and loss to new spring showers of hope.

Thanks also to friends who suggested favourites of their own, and to Penny, Deedee, Sheila and Wendy for allowing me to plunder their bookshelves.

I have discovered old friends and made new ones in these pages. I hope you will too.

Fiona Mackenzie Moore

ANONYMOUS

'Westron wind'

Westron wind, when wilt thou blow,
  The small rain down doth rain.
Christ, that my love were in my arms,
  And I in my bed again.

ANONYMOUS (c. 3rd century AD)

from **Pervigilium Veneris**
(The Night Watch of Venus)

May all love now, who never loved before;
May all who ever loved, now love the more.

Bright dayspring is here, and the budding earth
Brings forth fresh harmony in birth;
The songs of love unite all lovers true,
As the young birds choose their mates anew.
The trees grow fruit amid the warm rain,
And blossoms spread from glade to plain.
Now the Queen of Love walks the trees among,
And ties their tops with tresses strong,
And crowned upon her soft green throne
The laws of love she proclaims her own.

May all love now, who never loved before;
May all who ever loved, now love the more.

ANONYMOUS (16th century)

'Dear, if you change'

Dear, if you change, I'll never choose again.
Sweet, if you shrink, I'll never think of love.
Fair, if you fail, I'll judge all beauty vain.
Wise, if too weak, more wits I'll never prove.
Dear, Sweet, Fair, Wise, change, shrink, nor be not weak:
And, on my faith, my faith shall never break.

Earth with her flowers shall sooner heav'n adorn,
Heav'n her bright stars through earth's dim globe shall move,
Fire heat shall lose, and frosts of flames be born,
Air made to shine as black as hell shall prove:
Earth, Heaven, Fire, Air, the world transformed shall view,
Ere I prove false to faith, or strange to you.

FLEUR ADCOCK (born 1934)

Revision

It has to be learned afresh
every new start or every season,
revised like the languages that faltered
after I left school or when I stopped
going every year to Italy. Or
like how to float on my back, swimming,
not swimming, ears full of sea-water;
like the taste of the wine at first communion
(because each communion is the first);
like dancing and how to ride a horse -
can I still? Do I still want to?

The sun is on the leaves again;
birds are making rather special noises;
and I can see for miles and miles
even with my eyes closed.

So yes: teach it to me again.

MATTHEW ARNOLD (1822–1888)

'Below the Surface-Stream'

Below the surface-stream, shallow and light,
Of what we say we feel – below the stream,
As light, of what we think we feel – there flows
With noiseless current strong, obscure and deep,
The central stream of what we feel indeed.

To Marguerite – Continued

Yes! in the sea of life enisled,
With echoing straits between us thrown,
Dotting the shoreless watery wild,
We mortal millions live *alone*.
The islands feel the enclasping flow,
And then their endless bounds they know.

But when the moon their hollows lights,
And they are swept by balms of spring,
And in their glens, on starry nights,
The nightingales divinely sing;
And lovely notes, from shore to shore,
Across the sounds and channels pour–

Oh! then a longing like despair
Is to their farthest caverns sent;
For surely once, they feel, we were
Parts of a single continent!
Now round us spreads the watery plain–
Oh might our marges meet again!

Who ordered, that their longing's fire
Should be, as soon as kindled, cooled?
Who renders vain their deep desire?–
A God, a God their severance ruled!
And bade betwixt their shores to be
The unplumbed, salt, estranging sea.

W. H. AUDEN (1907–1973)

'Stop all the clocks'

Stop all the clocks, cut off the telephone,
Prevent the dog from barking with a juicy bone,
Silence the pianos and with muffled drum
Bring out the coffin, let the mourners come.

Let aeroplanes circle moaning overhead
Scribbling on the sky the message He Is Dead,
Put crêpe bows round the white necks of the public
    doves,
Let the traffic policemen wear black cotton gloves.

He was my North, my South, my East and West,
My working week and my Sunday rest,
My noon, my midnight, my talk, my song:
I thought that love would last for ever: I was wrong.

The stars are not wanted now: put out every one;
Pack up the moon and dismantle the sun;
Pour away the ocean and sweep up the wood;
For nothing now can ever come to any good.

'Warm are the still and lucky miles'

Warm are the still and lucky miles,
White shores of longing stretch away,
A light of recognition fills
    The whole great day, and bright
The tiny world of lovers' arms.

Silence invades the breathing wood
Where drowsy limbs a treasure keep,
Now greenly falls the learned shade
    Across the sleeping brows
And stirs their secret to a smile.

Restored! Returned! The lost are borne
On seas of shipwreck home at last:
See! In a fire of praising burns
    The dry dumb past, and we
Our life-day long shall part no more.

WILLIAM BARNES (1801–1886)

Woak[1] Hill

When sycamore leaves wer a-spreadèn
Green-ruddy in hedges,
Bezide the red doust[2] o' the ridges,
A-dried at Woak Hill;

I packed up my goods all a sheenèn[3]
Wi' long years o' handlèn,
On dousty red wheel ov a waggon,
To ride at Woak Hill.

The brown thatchen ruf o' the dwellèn,
I then wer a-leävèn,
Had shelter'd the sleek head o' Meäry,
My bride at Woak Hill.

But now vor zome years, her light voot-vall
'S a-lost vrom the vloorèn[4].
Too soon vor my jay[5] an' my childern,
She died at Woak Hill.

But still I do think that, in soul,
She do hover about us;
To ho[6] vor her motherless childern,
Her pride at Woak Hill.

Zoo[7]–lest she should tell me hereafter
I stole off 'ithout her,
An' left her, uncall'd at house-riddèn[8],
To bide at Woak Hill–

I call'd her so fondly, wi' lippèns[9]
All soundless to others,
An' took her wi' aïr-reachèn hand[10],
To my zide at Woak Hill.

On the road I did look round, a-talkèn
To light at my shoulder,
An' then led her in at the doorway,
Miles wide vrom Woak Hill.

An' that's why vo'k thought, vor a season,
My mind wer a-wandrèn
Wi' sorrow, when I wer so sorely
A-tried at Woak Hill.

But no; that my Meäry mid never
Behold herzelf slighted,
I wanted to think that I guided
My guide vrom Woak Hill.

[1] woak = oak. [2] doust = dust. [3] sheenèn = shining.
[4] vloorèn = floor. [5] jay = woman; [6] ho = watch over. [7] zoo = so.
[8] house-riddèn = moving house. [9] lippèns = intimacles.
[10] aïr-reachèn hand = ghostly hand.

APHRA BEHN (1640–1689)

Love Armed

Love in Fantastic Triumph sat,
Whilst bleeding Hearts around him flowed,
For whom Fresh pains he did create,
And strange Tyrannic power he showed;
From thy Bright Eyes he took his fire,
Which round about, in sport he hurled;
But 'twas from mine he took desire,
Enough to undo the Amorous World.
From me he took his sighs and tears,
From thee his Pride and Cruelty;
From me his Languishments and Fears,
And every Killing Dart from thee;
Thus thou and I, the God have armed,
And set him up a Deity;
But my poor Heart alone is harmed,
Whilst thine the Victor is, and free.

JOHN BETJEMAN (1906–1984)

In a Bath Teashop

'Let us not speak, for the love we bear one another -
    Let us hold hands and look.'
She, such a very ordinary little woman;
    He, such a thumping crook;
But both, for a moment, little lower than the angels
    In the teashop's ingle-nook.

EARLE BIRNEY (1904–1995)

From the hazel bough

He met a lady
　　on a lazy street
hazel eyes
　　and little plush feet

her legs swam by
　　like lovely trout
eyes were trees
　　where boys leant out

hands in the dark and
　　a river side
round breasts rising
　　with the finger's tide

she was plump as a finch
　　and live as a salmon
gay as silk and
　　proud as a Brahmin

they winked when they met
    and laughed when they parted
never took time
    to be brokenhearted

but no man sees
    where the trout lie now
or what leans out
    from the hazel bough

WILLIAM BLAKE (1757–1827)

'Never seek to tell thy love'

Never seek to tell thy love,
  Love that never told can be;
For the gentle wind does move
  Silently, invisibly.

I told my love, I told my love,
  I told her all my heart;
Trembling, cold, in ghastly fears,
  Ah! she doth depart!

Soon as she was gone from me
  A traveller came by,
Silently, invisibly –
  O, was no deny.

The Clod and the Pebble

Love seeketh not Itself to please,
Nor for itself hath any care;
But for another gives its ease,
And builds a Heaven in Hell's despair.

So sang a little Clod of Clay,
Trodden with the cattle's feet;
But a Pebble of the brook,
Warbled out these metres meet.

Love seeketh only Self to please,
To bind another to its delight:
Joys in anothers loss of ease,
And builds a Hell in Heaven's despite.

'How sweet I roamed'

How sweet I roamed from field to field
   And tasted all the summer's pride,
Till I the prince of love beheld
   Who in the sunny beams did glide!

He showed me lilies for my hair,
   And blushing roses for my brow;
He led me through his gardens fair
   Where all his golden pleasures grow.

With sweet May dews my wings were wet,
   And Phoebus fired my vocal rage;
He caught me in his silken net,
   And shut me in his golden cage.

He loves to sit and hear me sing,
   Then, laughing, sports and plays with me;
Then stretches out my golden wing,
   And mocks my loss of liberty.

FRANCIS WILLIAM BOURDILLON
(1852–1921)

'The night has a thousand eyes'

The night has a thousand eyes,
    And the day but one;
Yet the light of the bright world dies
    With the dying sun.

The mind has a thousand eyes,
    And the heart but one:
Yet the light of a whole life dies
    When love is done.

ANN BRADSTREET (1612–1672)

To my Dear and loving Husband

If ever two were one, then surely we.
If ever man were lov'd by wife, then thee
If ever wife was happy in a man,
Compare with me, ye women, if you can.
I prize thy love more than whole Mines of gold
Or all the riches that the East doth hold.
My love is such that Rivers cannot quench,
Nor ought but love from thee give recompence.
Thy love is such I can no way repay.
The heavens reward thee manifold, I pray.
Then while we live, in love let's so persever
That when we live no more, we may live ever.

CHRISTOPHER BRENNAN (1870–1932)

'My heart was wandering in the sands'

My heart was wandering in the sands,
a restless thing, a scorn apart;
Love set his fire in my hands,
I clasped the flame into my heart.

Surely, I said, my heart shall turn
one fierce delight of pointed flame;
and in that holocaust shall burn
its old unrest and scorn and shame:

Surely my heart the heavens at last
shall storm with fiery orisons,
and know, enthroned in the vast,
the fervid peace of molten suns.

The flame that feeds upon my heart
fades or flares, by wild winds controlled;
my heart still walks a thing apart,
my heart is restless as of old.

Because she would ask me why I loved her

If questioning would make us wise
No eyes would ever gaze in eyes;
If all our tale were told in speech
No mouths would wander each to each.

Were spirits free from mortal mesh
And love not bound in hearts of flesh
No aching breasts would yearn to meet
And find their ecstasy complete.

For who is there that lives and knows
The secret powers by which he grows?
Were knowledge all, what were our need
To thrill and faint and sweetly bleed?

Then seek not, sweet, the 'If' and 'Why'
I love you now until I die.
For I must love because I live
And life in me is what you give.

EMILY BRONTË (1818–1848)

from **Remembrance**

Cold in the earth – and the deep snow piled above
   thee,
   Far, far removed, cold in the dreary grave!
Have I forgot, my only Love, to love thee,
   Severed at last by Time's all-severing wave?

Now, when alone, do my thoughts no longer hover
   Over the mountains, on that northern shore,
Resting their wings where heath and fern-leaves
   cover
   Thy noble heart for ever, ever more?

Cold in the earth – and fifteen wild Decembers
   From these brown hills have melted into spring:
Faithful, indeed, is the spirit that remembers
   After such years of change and suffering!

Sweet Love of youth, forgive, if I forget thee,
  While the world's tide is bearing me along;
Other desires and other hopes beset me,
  Hopes which obscure, but cannot do thee wrong!

RUPERT BROOKE (1887–1915)

The One Before the Last

I dreamt I was in love again
      With the One Before the Last,
And smiled to greet the pleasant pain
      Of that innocent young past.

But I jumped to feel how sharp had been
      The pain when it did live,
How the faded dreams of Nineteen-ten
      Were Hell in Nineteen-five.

The boy's woe was as keen and clear,
      The boy's love just as true,
And the One Before the Last, my dear,
      Hurt quite as much as you.

Sickly I pondered how the lover
      Wrongs the unanswering tomb,
And sentimentalizes over
      What earned a better doom.

Gently he tombs the poor dim last time,
    Strews pinkish dust above,
And sighs, "The dear dead boyish pastime!
    But this – ah, God! – is Love!"

– Better oblivion hide dead true loves,
    Better the night enfold,
Than men, to eke the praise of new loves,
    Should lie about the old!

Oh! bitter thoughts I had in plenty.
    But here's the worst of it –
I shall forget, in Nineteen-twenty,
    You ever hurt a bit!

ELIZABETH BARRETT BROWNING
(1806–1861)

from **Sonnets from the Portuguese**

If thou must love me, let it be for nought
Except for love's sake only. Do not say,
'I love her for her smile – her look – her way
Of speaking gently – for a trick of thought
That falls in well with mine, and certes brought
A sense of pleasant ease on such a day.'
For these things in themselves, Belovèd, may
Be changed, or change for thee – and love, so
   wrought,
May be unwrought so. Neither love me for
Thine own dear pity's wiping my cheeks dry –
A creature might forget to weep, who bore
Thy comfort long, and lose thy love thereby!
But love me for love's sake, that evermore
Thou may'st love on, through love's eternity.

How do I love thee? Let me count the ways.
I love thee to the depth and breadth and height
My soul can reach, when feeling out of sight
For the ends of Being and ideal Grace.
I love thee to the level of every day's
Most quiet need, by sun and candlelight.
I love thee freely, as men strive for right;
I love thee purely, as they turn from praise.
I love thee with the passion put to use
In my old griefs, and with my childhood's faith.
I love thee with a love I seemed to lose
With my lost saints… I love thee with the breath,
Smiles, tears, of all my life!… and, if God choose,
I shall but love thee better after death.

And wilt thou have me fashion into speech
The love I bear thee, finding words enough,
And hold the torch out, while the winds are rough,
Between our faces, to cast light upon each?
I drop it at thy feet. I cannot teach
My hand to hold my spirit so far off
From myself… me… that I should bring thee proof,
In words of love hid in me… out of reach.
Nay, let the silence of my womanhood
Commend my woman-love to thy belief, –
Seeing that I stand unwon, however wooed,
And rend the garment of my life, in brief,
By a most dauntless, voiceless fortitude,
Lest one touch of this heart convey its grief

ROBERT BROWNING (1812–1889)

Meeting at Night

The gray sea and the long black land;
And the yellow half-moon large and low;
And the startled little waves that leap
In fiery ringlets from their sleep,
As I gain the cove with pushing prow,
And quench its speed i' the slushy sand.

Then a mile of warm sea-scented beach;
Three fields to cross till a farm appears;
A tap at the pane, the quick sharp scratch,
And blue spurt of a lighted match,
And a voice less loud, thro' its joys and fears,
Than the two hearts beating each to each!

The Lost Mistress

All's over, then: does truth sound bitter
As one at first believes?
Hark, 'tis the sparrows' good-night twitter
About your cottage eaves!

And the leaf-buds on the vine are woolly,
I noticed that, to-day;
One day more bursts them open fully
–You know the red turns grey.

To-morrow we meet the same then, dearest?
May I take your hand in mine?
Mere friends are we,–well, friends the merest
Keep much that I resign:

For each glance of the eye so bright and black,
Though I keep with heart's endeavour,–
Your voice, when you wish the snowdrops back,
Though it stay in my soul for ever!–

Yet I will but say what mere friends say,
Or only a thought stronger;
I will hold your hand but as long as all may,
Or so very little longer!

ROBERT BURNS (1759–1796)

'John Anderson, my jo'

John Anderson, my jo, John,[1]
   When we were first acquent,[2]
Your locks were like the raven,
   Your bonie brow was brent;[3]
But now your brow is bald, John,
   Your locks are like the snow;
But blessings on your frosty pow,[4]
   John Anderson, my jo.

John Anderson, my jo, John,
   We clamb the hill thegither;
And mony a cantie day, John,[5]
   We've had wi' ane anither:[6]
Now we maun totter down, John;
   But hand in hand we'll go,
And sleep thegither at the foot,
   John Anderson, my jo.

[1] jo = sweetheart. [2] acquent = acquainted. [3] brent = smooth.
[4] pow = head. [5] cantie = cheerful. [6] ane anither = one another.

'O wert thou in the cauld blast'

O wert thou in the cauld blast,
  On yonder lea, on yonder lea,
My plaidie to the angry airt,[1]
  I'd shelter thee, I'd shelter thee.

Or did misfortune's bitter storms
  Around thee blaw, around thee blaw,
Thy bield should be my bosom,[2]
  To share it a', to share it a'!

O were I in the wildest waste,
  Sae black and bare, sae black and bare,
The desert were a Paradise,
  If thou wert there, if thou wert there;

Or were I monarch o' the globe,
  Wi' thee to reign, wi' thee to reign,
The brightest jewel in my crown
  Wad be my queen, wad be my queen!

[1] plaidie = shawl; airt = quarter. [2] bield = shelter, refuge.

My Luve

O my Luve is like a red, red rose
    That's newly sprung in June:
O my Luve is like the melodie,
    That's sweetly play'd in tune.

As fair art thou, my bonie lass,
    So deep in luve am I;
And I will luve thee still, my dear,
    Till a' the seas gang dry.

Till a' the seas gang dry, my dear,
    And the rocks melt wi' the sun;
I will luve thee still, my dear,
    While the sands o' life shall run.

And fare thee weel, my only Luve!
    And fare thee weel awhile!
And I will come again, my Luve,
    Tho' it were ten thousand mile.

GEORGE GORDON, LORD BYRON
(1788–1824)

'She walks in beauty'
(from 'Hebrew Melodies')

She walks in beauty, like the night
Of cloudless climes and starry skies,
And all that's best of dark and bright
Meet in her aspect and her eyes;
Thus mellowed to that tender light
Which heaven to gaudy day denies.

One shade the more, one ray the less,
Had half impaired the nameless grace
Which waves in every raven tress
Or softly lightens o'er her face;
Where thoughts serenely sweet express
How pure, how dear their dwelling-place.

And on that cheek, and o'er that brow,
So soft, so calm, yet eloquent,
The smiles that win, the tints that glow

But tell of days in goodness spent,
A mind at peace with all below,
A heart whose love is innocent!

We'll go no more a-roving

So, we'll go no more a-roving
   So late into the night,
Though the heart be still as loving,
   And the moon be still as bright.

For the sword outwears its sheath,
   And the soul wears out the breast,
And the heart must pause to breathe,
   And love itself have rest.

Though the night was made for loving,
   And the day returns too soon,
Yet we'll go no more a-roving
   By the light of the moon.

from **Don Juan**

194

'Man's love is of man's life a thing apart,
    'Tis woman's whole existence; man may range
The court, camp, church, the vessel, and the mart;
    Sword, gown, gain, glory, offer in exchange
Pride, fame, ambition, to fill up his heart,
    And few there are whom these cannot estrange;
Men have all these resources, we but one,
    To love again, and be again undone.

195

'You will proceed in pleasure, and in pride,
    Beloved and loving many; all is o'er
For me on earth, except some years to hide
    My shame and sorrow deep in my heart's core;
These I could bear, but cannot cast aside
    The passion which still rages as before –
And so farewell – forgive me, love me – No,
    That word is idle now – but let it go.

196

'My breast has been all weakness, is so yet;
    But still I think I can collect my mind;
My blood still rushes where my spirit's set,
    As roll the waves before the settled wind;
My heart is feminine, nor can forget –
    To all, except one image, madly blind;
So shakes the needle, and so stands the pole,
    As vibrates my fond heart to my fixed soul.

197

'I have no more to say, but linger still,
    And dare not set my seal upon this sheet,
And yet I may as well the task fulfil,
    My misery can scarce be more complete:
I had not lived till now, could sorrow kill;
    Death shuns the wretch who fain the blow would
    meet,
And I must even survive this last adieu,
    And bear with life, to love and pray for you!'

THOMAS CAMPION (c.1567–1620)

'Follow your saint'

Follow your saint, follow with accents sweet!
Haste you, sad notes, fall at her flying feet!
There, wrapt in cloud of sorrow, pity move,
And tell the ravisher of my soul I perish for her love:
But if she scorns my never-ceasing pain,
Then burst with sighing in her sight, and ne'er return
   again!

All that I sung still to her praise did tend;
Still she was first, still she my songs did end;
Yet she my love and music both doth fly,
The music that her echo is and beauty's sympathy:
Then let my notes pursue her scornful flight!
It shall suffice that they were breathed and died for
   her delight.

'Kind are her answers'

Kind are her answers,
But her performance keeps no day ;
Breaks time, as dancers
From their own Music when they stray :
All her free favours and smooth words,
Wing my hopes in vain.
O did ever voice so sweet but only fain?
Can true love yield such delay,
Converting joy to pain?

Lost is our freedom
When we submit to women so:
Why do we need them,
When in their best they work our woe?
There is no wisdom
Can alter ends, by Fate prefixt.
O why is the good of man with evil mixed?
Never were days yet called two,
But one night went betwixt.

RAYMOND CARVER (1938–1988)

Late Fragment

And did you get what
you wanted from this life, even so?
I did.
And what did you want?
To call myself beloved, to feel myself
beloved on the earth.

JOHN CLARE (1793–1864)

To Mary

I sleep with thee, and wake with thee,
And yet thou art not there;
I fill my arms with thoughts of thee,
And press the common air.

Thy eyes are gazing upon mine
When thou art out of sight;
My lips are always touching thine
At morning, noon, and night.

I think and speak of other things
To keep my mind at rest,
But still to thee my memory clings
Like love in woman's breast.

I hide it from the world's wide eye
And think and speak contrary,
But soft the wind comes from the sky
And whispers tales of Mary.

The night-wind whispers in my ear,
The moon shines on my face;
The burden still of chilling fear
I find in every place.

The breeze is whispering in the bush,
And the leaves fall from the tree,
All sighing on, and will not hush,
Some pleasant tales of thee.

First Love

I ne'er was struck before that hour
With love so sudden and so sweet.
Her face it bloomed like a sweet flower
And stole my heart away complete.

My face turned pale, a deadly pale.
My legs refused to walk away,
And when she looked what could I ail
My life and all seemed turned to clay.

And then my blood rushed to my face
And took my eyesight quite away.
The trees and bushes round the place
Seemed midnight at noonday.

I could not see a single thing,
Words from my eyes did start.
They spoke as chords do from the string,
And blood burnt round my heart.

Are flowers the winter's choice
Is love's bed always snow
She seemed to hear my silent voice
Not love's appeals to know.

I never saw so sweet a face
As that I stood before.
My heart has left its dwelling place
And can return no more.

SAMUEL TAYLOR COLERIDGE
(1772–1834)

Desire

Where true Love burns Desire is Love's pure flame;
It is the reflex of our earthly frame,
That takes its meaning from the nobler part,
And but translates the language of the heart.

WILLIAM CONGREVE (1670–1729)

Song

False though she be to me and love,
  I'll ne'er pursue revenge;
For still the charmer I approve,
  Though I deplore her change.

In hours of bliss we oft have met:
  They could not always last;
And though the present I regret,
  I'm grateful for the past.

WENDY COPE (born 1945)

Bloody Men

Bloody men are like bloody buses –
You wait for about a year –
And as soon as one approaches your stop
Two or three others appear.

You look at them flashing their indicators,
Offering you a ride.
You're trying to read the destinations,
You haven't much time to decide.

If you make a mistake, there is no turning back.
Jump off, and you'll stand there and gaze
While the cars and taxis and lorries go by
And the minutes, the hours, the days.

EMILY DICKINSON (1830–1886)

Love's stricken 'why'

Love's stricken 'why'
Is all that love can speak –
Built of but just a syllable
The hugest hearts that break.

'I gave myself to Him'

I gave myself to him
And took himself for pay.
The solemn contract of a life
Was ratified this way

The value might disappoint
Myself a poorer prove
Than this my purchaser suspect
The daily own of love.

Depreciates the sight
But, 'til the merchant buy,
Still fabled, in the isles of spice
The subtle cargoes lie.

At least, 'tis mutual risk'
(Some found it mutual gain)
Sweet debt of life-each night to owe,
Insolvent every noon!

JOHN DONNE (1573–1631)

To His Mistress Going to Bed
(from 'Elegy 19')

Come, Madam, come, all rest my powers defy,
Until I labour, I in labour lie.
The foe oft-times having the foe in sight,
Is tired with standing though he never fight.
Off with that girdle, like heaven's Zone glistering,
But a far fairer world encompassing.
Unpin that spangled breastplate which you wear,
That the eyes of busy fools may be stopt there.
Unlace yourself, for that harmonious chime
Tells me from you, that now it is bed time.
Off with that happy busk, which I envy,
That still can be, and still can stand so nigh.
Your gown going off, such beauteous state reveals,
As when from flowery meads th' hill's shadow steals....

    Licence my roving hands, and let them go,
Before, behind, between, above, below.
O my America! my new-found-land,
My kingdom, safeliest when with one man manned,

My Mine of precious stones, my Empery,
How blest am I in this discovering thee!
To enter in these bonds, is to be free;
Then where my hand is set, my seal shall be.
   Full nakedness! All joys are due to thee,
As souls unbodied, bodies unclothed must be,
To taste whole joys. Gems which you women use
Are like Atlanta's ball cast in men's views ;
That, when a fool's eye lighteth on a gem,
His earthly soul might court that, not them.
Like pictures, or like books' gay coverings made
For laymen, are all women thus array'd.
Themselves are only mystic books, which we
-Whom their imputed grace will dignify-
Must see reveal'd. Then, since that I may know,
As liberally as to thy midwife show
Thyself ; cast all, yea, this white linen hence ;
There is no penance due to innocence :
To teach thee, I am naked first ; why then,
What needst thou have more covering than a man?

'Go and catch a falling star'

Go and catch a falling star,
Get with child a mandrake root,
Tell me where all past years are,
Or who cleft the Devil's foot,
Teach me to hear mermaids singing,
Or to keep off envy's stinging,
    And find
    What wind
Serves to advance an honest mind.

If thou be'st born to strange sights,
Things invisible to see,
Ride ten thousand days and nights,
Till age snow white hairs on thee;
Thou, when thou return'st, wilt tell me
All strange wonders that befell thee,
    And swear
    No where
Lives a woman true, and fair.

If thou find'st one, let me know,
Such a pilgrimage were sweet;
Yet do not, I would not go,
Though at next door we might meet:
Though she were true, when you met her,
And last, till you write your letter,
Yet she
Will be
False, ere I come, to two or three.

A Valediction, Forbidding Mourning

As virtuous men pass mildly away,
And whisper to their souls to go,
Whilst some of their sad friends do say,
'Now his breath goes,' and some say, 'No.'

So let us melt, and make no noise,
No tear-floods, nor sigh-tempests move;
'Twere profanation of our joys
To tell the laity our love.

Moving of th' earth brings harms and fears;
Men reckon what it did, and meant;
But trepidation of the spheres,
Though greater far, is innocent.

Dull sublunary lovers' love
– Whose soul is sense – cannot admit
Of absence, 'cause it doth remove
The thing which elemented it.

But we by a love so much refined,
That ourselves know not what it is,
Inter-assurèd of the mind,
Care less, eyes, lips and hands to miss.

Our two souls therefore, which are one,
Though I must go, endure not yet
A breach, but an expansion,
Like gold to aery thinness beat.

If they be two, they are two so
As stiff twin compasses are two;
Thy soul, the fix'd foot, makes no show
To move, but doth, if th' other do.

And though it in the centre sit,
Yet, when the other far doth roam,
It leans, and hearkens after it,
And grows erect, as that comes home.

Such wilt thou be to me, who must,
Like th' other foot, obliquely run;
Thy firmness makes my circle just,
And makes me end where I begun.

JOHN DOWLAND (1563–1626)

'Weep you no more, sad fountains'

Weep you no more, sad fountains;
    What need you flow so fast?
Look how the snowy mountains
    Heaven's sun doth gently waste.
But my sun's heavenly eyes
    View not your weeping,
    That now lies sleeping
Softly, now softly lies sleeping.

Sleep is a reconciling,
    A rest that peace begets:
Doth not the sun rise smiling
    When fair at even he sets?
Rest you then, rest, sad eyes,
    Melt not in weeping,
    While she lies sleeping
Softly, now softly lies sleeping.

ERNEST DOWSON (1867–1900)

Days of Wine and Roses

Vitae Summa Brevis Spem Nos Vetat Incohare Longam

They are not long, the weeping and the laughter,
Love and desire and hate:
I think they have no portion in us after
We pass the gate.

They are not long, the days of wine and roses:
Out of a misty dream
Our path merges for a while, then closes
Within a dream.

MICHAEL DRAYTON (1563–1631)

Parting

Since there's no help, come let us kiss and part;
Nay, I have done, you get no more of me;
And I am glad, yea glad with all my heart,
That thus so cleanly I myself can free.

Shake hands for ever, cancel all our vows,
And, when we meet at any time again,
Be it not seen in either of our brows
That we one jot of former love retain.

Now at the last gasp of Love's latest breath,
When, his pulse failing, Passion speechless lies,
When Faith is kneeling by his bed of death,
And Innocence is closing up his eyes –
  Now, if thou wouldst, when all have given him over,
  From death to life thou might'st him yet recover!

SIR EDWARD DYER (1543–1607)

Love is love

The lowest trees have tops, the ant her gall,
The fly her spleen, the little spark his heat,
And slender hairs cast shadows though but small,
And bees have stings although they be not great.
Seas have their source, and so have shallow springs,
And love is love in beggars and in kings.

Where waters smoothest run, deep are the fords,
The dial stirs, yet none perceives it move:
The firmest faith is in the fewest words,
The turtles[1] cannot sing, and yet they love,
True hearts have eyes and ears no tongues to speak:
They hear, and see, and sigh, and then they break.

[1] 'turtles' = 'turtledoves'

T. S. ELIOT (1888–1965)

la figlia che piange
O Quam Te Memorem Virgo …

Stand on the highest pavement of the stair –
Lean on a garden urn –
Weave, weave the sunlight in your hair –
Clasp your flowers to you with a pained surprise –
Fling them to the ground and turn
With a fugitive resentment in your eyes:
But weave, weave the sunlight in your hair.

So I would have had him leave,
So I would have had her stand and grieve,
So he would have left
As the soul leaves the body torn and bruised,
As the mind deserts the body it has used.
I should find
Some way incomparably light and deft,
Some way we both should understand,
Simple and faithless as a smile and shake of the hand.

She turned away, but with the autumn weather
Compelled my imagination many days,
Many days and many hours:
Her hair over her arms and her arms full of flowers.
And I wonder how they should have been together!
I should have lost a gesture and a pose.
Sometimes these cogitations still amaze
The troubled midnight and the noon's repose.

RALPH WALDO EMERSON (1803–1882)

Give All to Love

Give all to love;
Obey thy heart;
Friends, kindred, days,
Estate, good-fame,
Plans, credit, and the Muse,–
Nothing refuse.
'Tis a brave master;
Let it have scope:
Follow it utterly,
Hope beyond hope:
High and more high
It dives into noon,
With wing unspent,
Untold intent;
But it is a God,
Knows its own path
And the outlets of the sky.
It was never for the mean;
It requireth courage stout.

Souls above doubt,
Valor unbending,
It will reward,–
They shall return
More than they were,
And ever ascending.
Leave all for love;
Yet, hear me, yet,
One word more thy heart behoved,
One pulse more of firm endeavor,–
Keep thee to-day,
To-morrow, forever,
Free as an Arab
Of thy beloved.
Cling with life to the maid;
But when the surprise,
First vague shadow of surmise
Flits across her bosom young,
Of a joy apart from thee,
Free be she, fancy-free;
Nor thou detain her vesture's hem,
Nor the palest rose she flung
From her summer diadem.

Though thou loved her as thyself,
As a self of purer clay,
Though her parting dims the day,
Stealing grace from all alive;
Heartily know,
When half-gods go,
The gods survive.

U. A. FANTHORPE (born 1929)

Going Under

I turn over pages, you say,
Louder than any woman in Europe.

But reading's my specific for keeping
Reality at bay; my lullaby.

You slip into sleep as fast
And neat as a dipper.
You lie there breathing, breathing.

My language is turn over
Over and over again. I am a fish
Netted on giveaway mattress,
Urgent to be out of the air.

Reading would help; or pills.
But light would wake you from your resolute
Progress through night.

The dreams waiting for me twitter and bleat.
All the things I ever did wrong
Queue by the bed in order of precedence,
Worst last.

Exhausted by guilt, I nuzzle
Your shoulder. Out lobs
A casual, heavy arm. You anchor me
In your own easy sound.

EDWARD FITZGERALD (1809–93)

from **The Rubaiyat of Omar Khayyam**

10

With me along some Strip of Herbage strown
That just divides the desert from the sown,
   Where name of Slave and Sultán scarce is known,
And pity Sultán Mahmud on his Throne.

11

Here with a Loaf of Bread beneath the Bough,
A Flask of Wine, a Book of Verse – and Thou
   Beside me singing in the Wilderness –
And Wilderness is Paradise enow.

THOMAS FLATMAN (1637–1688)

An Appeal to Cats in the
Business of Love

Ye cats that at midnight spit love at each other
Who best feel the pangs of a passionate lover,
I appeal to your scratches and your tattered fur,
If the business of love be no more than to purr.
Old Lady Grimalkin with her gooseberry eyes
Knew some thing when a kitten, for why she was
wise;
You find by experience, the love-fit's soon o'er,
Puss! Puss! lasts not long, but turns to Cat-whore!

Men ride many miles
Cats tread many tiles,
Both hazard their necks in the fray;
Only cats, when they fall
From a house or a wall,
Keep their feet, mount their tails, and away!

JOHN FLETCHER (1579–1625)

'Take, oh, take those lips away'

Take, oh, take those lips away
   That so sweetly were forsworn,
And those eyes, like break of day,
   Lights that do mislead the morn;
But my kisses bring again,
   Seals of love, though sealed in vain.

Hide, oh, hide those hills of snow,
   Which thy frozen bosom bears,
On whose tops the pinks that grow
   Are of those that April wears.
But first set my poor heart free,
   Bound in those icy chains by thee.

JOHN GAY (1685–1732)

'Over the hills and far away'
(from 'The Beggar's Opera')

Macheath
Were I laid on Greenland's coast,
And in my arms embraced my lass;
Warm amidst eternal frost,
Too soon the half year's night would pass.

Polly
Were I sold on Indian soil,
Soon as the burning day was closed,
I could mock the sultry toil
When on my charmer's breast reposed.

Macheath
And I would love you all the day,

Polly
Every night would kiss and play,

Macheath
If with me you'd fondly stray

Polly
Over the hills and far away.

W. S. GILBERT (1836–1911)

from **Trial By Jury**

When I, good friends, was called to the bar,
I'd an appetite fresh and hearty.
But I was, as many young barristers are,
An impecunious party.
I'd a swallow-tail coat of a beautiful blue–
And a brief which I bought of a booby–
A couple of shirts, and a collar or two,
And a ring that looked like a ruby!

CHORUS
A couple of shirts, and a collar or two,
And a ring that looked like a ruby!

JUDGE
In Westminster Hall I danced a dance,
Like a semi-despondent fury;
For I thought I never should hit on a chance
Of addressing a British Jury–
But I soon got tired of third-class journeys,
And dinners of bread and water;

So I fell in love with a rich attorney's
Elderly, ugly daughter.

CHORUS·
So he fell in love with a rich attorney's
Elderly, ugly daughter.

JUDGE
The rich attorney, he jumped with joy,
And replied to my fond professions:
'You shall reap the reward of your pluck, my boy,
At the Bailey and Middlesex sessions.
You'll soon get used to her looks,' said he,
'And a very nice girl you'll find her!
She may very well pass for forty-three
In the dusk, with a light behind her!'

CHORUS
She may very well pass for forty-three
In the dusk, with a light behind her!

JUDGE
The rich attorney was good as his word;
The briefs came trooping gaily,
And every day my voice was heard
At the Sessions or Ancient Bailey.

All thieves who could my fees afford
Relied on my orations.
And many a burglar I've restored
To his friends and his relations.

CHORUS
And many a burglar he's restored
To his friends and his relations.

JUDGE
At length I became as rich as the Gurneys–
An incubus then I thought her,
So I threw over that rich attorney's
Elderly, ugly daughter.
The rich attorney my character high
Tried vainly to disparage--
And now, if you please, I'm ready to try
This Breach of Promise of Marriage!

CHORUS
And now if you please, he's ready to try
This Breach of Promise of Marriage!

JOHANN WOLFGANG VON GOETHE
(1749–1832)

Night Thoughts

Oh, unhappy stars! your fate I mourn,

Ye by whom the sea-tossed sailor's lighted,
Who with radiant beams the heav'ns adorn,

But by gods and men are unrequited:
For ye love not,–ne'er have learnt to love!
Ceaselessly in endless dance ye move,
In the spacious sky your charms displaying,

What far travels ye have hastened through,
Since, within my loved one's arms delaying,

I've forgotten you and midnight too!

JAMES GRAHAM, MARQUIS OF MONTROSE (1612–1650)

'My dear and only Love'

My dear and only Love, I pray
   That little world of thee
Be govern'd by no other sway
   Than purest monarchy;
For if confusion have a part
   (Which virtuous souls abhor),
And hold a synod in thine heart,
   I'll never love thee more.

Like Alexander I will reign,
   And I will reign alone;
My thoughts did evermore disdain
   A rival on my throne.
He either fears his fate too much,
   Or his deserts are small,
That dares not put it to the touch,
   To gain or lose it all.

And in the empire of thine heart,
  Where I should solely be,
If others do pretend a part
  Or dare to vie with me,
Or if Committees thou erect,
  And go on such a score,
I'll laugh and sing at thy neglect,
  And never love thee more.

But if thou wilt prove faithful then,
  And constant of thy word,
I'll make thee glorious by my pen
  And famous by my sword;
I'll serve thee in such noble ways
  Was never heard before;
I'll crown and deck thee all with bays,
  And love thee more and more.

ROBERT GRAVES (1895–1985)

'She tells her love while half asleep'

She tells her love while half asleep,
In the dark hours,
  With half-words whispered low:
As Earth stirs in her winter sleep
  And puts out grass and flowers
    Despite the snow,
    Despite the falling snow.

A Slice of Wedding Cake

Why have such scores of lovely, gifted girls
  Married impossible men?
Simple self-sacrifice may be ruled out,
  And missionary endeavour, nine times out of ten.

Repeat 'impossible men': not merely rustic,
   Foul-tempered or depraved
(Dramatic foils chosen to show the world
   How well women behave, and always have
    behaved).

Impossible men: idle, illiterate,
   Self-pitying, dirty, sly,
For whose appearance even in City parks
   Excuses must be made to casual passers-by.

Has God's supply of tolerable husbands
   Fallen, in fact, so low?
Or do I always over-value woman
   At the expense of man?
     Do I?
       It might be so.

IVOR GURNEY (1890–1937)

'My heart makes songs on lonely roads'

My heart makes songs on lonely roads
To comfort me while you're away,
And strives with lovely sounding words
its crowded tenderness to say.

Glimmering against the forward dark,
Your face I see with pride, with pain
So that one time I did desire
Never to see that face again.

But I am glad that Love has come
To bind me fast and try my worth;
For love's a powerful Lord and gives
His friends dominion over the earth.

THOMAS HARDY (1840–1928)

At Tea

The kettle descants in a cosy drone,
And the young wife looks in her husband's face,
And then at her guest's, and shows in her own
Her sense that she fills an envied place;
And the visiting lady is all abloom,
And says there was never so sweet a room.

And the happy young housewife does not know
That the woman beside her was first his choice,
Till the fates ordained it could not be so…
Betraying nothing in look or voice
The guest sits smiling and sips her tea,
And he throws her a stray glance yearningly.

A Thunderstorm in Town
(A Reminiscence, 1893)

She wore a 'terra-cotta' dress,
And we stayed, because of the pelting storm,
Within the hansom's dry recess,
Though the horse had stopped; yea, motionless
We sat on, snug and warm.

Then the downpour ceased, to my sharp sad pain,
And the glass that had screened our forms before
Flew up, and out she sprang to her door:
I should have kissed her if the rain
Had lasted a minute more.

ROBERT HERRICK (1591–1674)

Upon Love

Love brought me to a silent grove,
  And showed me there a tree,
Where some had hanged themselves for love,
  And gave a twist to me.

The halter was of silk and gold,
  That he reached forth unto me:
No otherwise, than if he would
  By dainty things undo me.

He bade me then that necklace use;
  And told me too, he maketh
A glorious end by such a noose,
  His death for love that taketh.

'Twas but a dream. But had I been
  There rèally alone,
My desperate fears, in love, had seen
  Mine execuòtn.

Upon Julia's Clothes

Whenas in silks my Julia goes
Then, then (methinks) how sweetly flows
That liquefaction of her clothes.

Next, when I cast mine eyes, and see
That brave vibration each way free;
O how that glittering taketh me!

To the Virgins, to Make Much of Time

Gather ye rosebuds while ye may,
Old Time is still a-flying:
And this same flower that smiles today
Tomorrow will be dying.

The glorious lamp of heaven, the Sun,
The higher he's a-getting
The sooner will his race be run,
And nearer he's to setting.

'White in the moon the long road lies'

White in the moon the long road lies,
  The moon stands blank above;
White in the moon the long road lies
  That leads me from my love.

Still hangs the hedge without a gust,
  Still, still the shadows stay:
My feet upon the moonlit dust
  Pursue the ceaseless way.

The world is round, so travellers tell,
  And straight though reach the track,
Trudge on, trudge on, 'twill all be well,
  The way will guide one back.

But ere the circle homeward hies
  Far, far must it remove:
White in the moon the long road lies
  That leads me from my love.

That age is best which is the first,
When youth and blood are warmer;
But being spent, the worse, and worst
Times still succeed the former.

Then be not coy, but use your time;
And while ye may, go marry:
For having lost but once your prime,
You may forever tarry.

Be My Mistress Short or Tall

Be my mistress short or tall
And distorted therewithall
Be she likewise one of those
That an acre hath of nose
Be her teeth ill hung or set
And her grinders black as jet
Be her cheeks so shallow too
As to show her tongue wag through
Hath she thin hair, hath she none
She's to me a paragon.

A. E. HOUSMAN (1859–1936)

'Because I liked you better'

Because I liked you better
Than suits a man to say,
It irked you, and I promised
To throw the thought away.

To put the world between us
We parted, stiff and dry;
'Good-bye', said you, 'forget me.'
'I will, no fear,' said I.

If here, where clover whitens
The dead man's knoll, you pass,
And no tall flower to meet you
Starts in the trefoiled grass,

Halt by the headstone naming
The heart no longer stirred,
And say the lad that loved you
Was one that kept his word.

'Oh, when I was in love with yo

Oh, when I was in love with you,
   Then I was clean and brave,
And miles around the wonder grew
   How well did I behave.

And now the fancy passes by,
   And nothing will remain,
And miles around they'll say that I
   Am quite myself again.

LEIGH HUNT (1784–1859)

'Jenny kissed me'

Jenny kissed me when we met,
  Jumping from the chair she sat in;
Time, you thief, who love to get
  Sweets into your list, put that in!

Say I'm weary, say I'm sad,
  Say that health and wealth have missed me,
Say I'm growing old, but add,
  Jenny kissed me.

BEN JONSON (1572–1637)

Sweet Neglect

Still to be neat, still to be drest,
As you were going to a feast:
Still to be powdered, still perfumed:
Lady, it is to be presumed.
Though art's hid causes are not found,
All is not sweet, all is not sound.

Give me a look, give me a face
That makes simplicity a grace;
Robes loosely flowing, hair as free:
Such sweet neglect more taketh me,
Than all th' adulteries of art,
That strike mine eyes, but not my heart.

'Doing, a filthy pleasure is'
(from the Latin of Petronius)

Doing, a filthy pleasure is, and short;
And done, we straight repent us of the sport:
Let us not rush blindly on unto it,
Like lustful beasts, that only know to do it:
For lust will languish, and that heat decay,
But thus, thus, keeping endless Holy-day,
Let us together closely lie, and kiss,
There is no labour, nor no shame in this;
This hath pleased, doth please and long will please; never
Can this decay, but is beginning ever.

JOHN KEATS (1795–1821)

Bright Star

Bright Star, would I were steadfast as thou art–
Not in lone splendour hung aloft the night,
And watching, with eternal lids apart,
Like Nature's patient sleepless Eremite,
The moving waters at their priest-like task
Of pure ablution round earth's human shores,
Or gazing on the new soft-fallen mask
Of snow upon the mountains and the moors–
No-yet still steadfast, still unchangeable,
Pillow'd upon my fair love's ripening breast,
To feel for ever its soft fall and swell,
Awake for ever in a sweet unrest,
Still, still to hear her tender-taken breath,
And so live ever- or else swoon to death.

'This living hand'

This living hand, now warm and capable
Of earnest grasping, would, if it were cold
And in the icy silence of the tomb,
So haunt thy days and chill thy dreaming nights
That thou would wish thine own heart dry of blood
So in my veins red life might stream again,
And thou be conscience-calmed – see here it is –
I hold it towards you.

WALTER SAVAGE LANDOR (1775–1864)

'Mother, I cannot mind my wheel'

Mother, I cannot mind my wheel;
    My fingers ache, my lips are dry;
O, if you felt the pain I feel!
    But O, who ever felt as I!
No longer could I doubt him true –
    All other men may use deceit.
He always said my eyes were blue,
    And often swore my lips were sweet.

Heartsease

There is a flower I wish to wear
But not until first worn by you –
Heartsease – of all earth's flowers most rare;
Bring it; and bring enough for two.

PHILIP LARKIN (1922–1985)

'The little lives of earth and form'

The little lives of earth and form,
 Of finding food, and keeping warm,
  Are not like ours, and yet
A kinship lingers nonetheless:
We hanker for the homeliness
  Of den, and hole, and set.

And this identity we feel
– Perhaps not right, perhaps not real –
  Will link us constantly;
I see the rock, the clay, the chalk,
The flattened grass, the swaying stalk,
  And it is you I see.

D. H. LAWRENCE (1885–1930)

On the Balcony

In front of the sombre mountains,
a faint, lost ribbon of rainbow
And between us and it, the thunder;
And down below in the green wheat,
the labourers stand like dark stumps,
still in the green wheat.

You are near to me, and naked feet
In their sandals, and through the
scent of the balcony's naked timber
I distinguish the scent of your hair:
so now the limber

Lightning falls from heaven.
Adown the pale-green glacier river floats
A dark boat through the gloom—
and whither? The thunder roars

But still we have each other!
The naked lightnings in the heavens dither
And disappear–
what have we but each other?
The boat has gone.

T. E. LAWRENCE (1888–1935)

Dedication to Seven Pillars of Wisdom

To S.A.

I loved you, so I drew these tides of men into my hands
and wrote my will across the sky in stars
To earn you Freedom, the seven-pillared worthy house,
that your eyes might be shining for me
When we came.

Death seemed my servant on the road, till we were near
and saw you waiting:
When you smiled, and in sorrowful envy he outran me
and took you apart·
Into his quietness.

Love, the way-weary, groped to your body,
our brief wage
ours for the moment
Before earth's soft hand explored your shape,
and the blind
worms grew fat upon
Your substance.

Men prayed me that I set our work, the inviolate house,
as a memory of you.
But for fit monument I shattered it, unfinished: and now
The little things creep out to patch themselves hovels
in the marred shadow
Of your gift.

C. S. LEWIS (1898–1963)

As the Ruin Falls

All this is flashy rhetoric about loving you.
I never had a selfless thought since I was born.
I am mercenary and self-seeking through and through:
I want God, you, all friends, merely to serve my turn.

Peace, re-assurance, pleasure, are the goals I seek,
I cannot crawl one inch outside my proper skin:
I talk of love –a scholar's parrot may talk Greek–
But, self-imprisoned, always end where I begin.

Only that now you have taught me (but how late)
    my lack.
I see the chasm. And everything you are was making
My heart into a bridge by which I might get back
From exile, and grow man. And now the bridge is
    breaking.

For this I bless you as the ruin falls. The pains
You give me are more precious than all other gains.

LIZ LOCHHEAD (born 1947)

Sundaysong

its about time
it came back again
if it was going to.
yes   something's nesting
in the tentative creeper scribbling
Kellygreen felt tip
across our bedroom window.
hello.
its a lovely morning.   we've got
full french roast for the enamelled yellow coffee pot.
there'll be transistors in the botanics
and blaring notes of blossom.
let's walk.   let's talk.
let the weekend watch wind down.
let there be sun
let first you and me
and then breakfast and lunch be
rolled into one.

RICHARD LOVELACE (1618–1658)

To Althea from Prison

When Love with unconfinèd wings
    Hovers within my gates,
And my divine Althea brings
    To whisper at the grates;
When I lie tangled in her hair
    And fettered to her eye,
The birds that wanton in the air
    Know no such liberty.

When flowing cups run swiftly round
    With no allaying Thames,
Our careless heads with roses crowned,
    Our hearts with loyal flames;
When thirsty grief in wine we steep,
    When healths and draughts go free,
Fishes that tipple in the deep
    Know no such liberty.

When, like committed linnets,
   With shriller throat shall sing
The sweetness, mercy, majesty,
   And glories of my King;
When I shall voice aloud how good
   He is, how great should be,
Enlargèd winds, that curl the flood
   Know no such liberty.

Stone walls do not a prison make,
   Nor iron bars a cage;
Minds innocents and quiet take
   That for an hermitage;
If I have freedom in my love
   And in my soul am free,
Angels alone, that soar above,
   Enjoy such liberty.

NORMAN MACCAIG (1910–1996)

Water Tap

There was this hayfield,
You remember, pale gold
If it weren't hazel
with a million cloven heads.

A rope of water
Frayed down – the bucket
Hoisted up a plate
Of flashing light.

The thin road screwed
Into hills; all ended
Journeys were somewhere,
But far, far.

You laughed, by the fence;
And everything that was
Hoisting water
Suddenly spilled over.

SORLEY MACLEAN (1911–1996)

from **Poems to Eimhir**

XVII
Multitude of the skies,
golden riddle of millions of stars,
cold, distant, lustrous, beautiful,
silent, unfeeling, unwelcoming.

Fullness of knowledge in their course,
emptiness of chartless ignorance,
a universe moving in silence,
a mind alone in its bounds.

Not they moved my thoughts,
not the marvel of their chill course,
to us there is no miracle but in love,
lighting of a universe in the kindling of your face.

ROGER McGOUGH (born 1935)

Ten Milk Bottles

ten milk bottles standing in the hall
ten milk bottles up against the wall
next door neighbour thinks we're dead
hasnt heard a sound he said
doesn't know we've been in bed
the ten whole days since we were wed

noone knows and noone sees
we lovers doing as we please
but people stop and point at these
ten milk bottles a-turning into cheese

ten milk bottles standing day and night
ten different thicknesses and
different shades of white
persistent carolsingers without a note to utter
silent carolsingers a-turning into butter

now she's run out of passion
and theres not much left in me
so maybe we'll get up
and make a cup of tea
then people can stop wondering
what they're waiting for
those ten milk bottles a-queuing at our door
those ten milk bottles a-queuing at our door

MARGARET, DUCHESS OF NEWCASTLE
(1623–1673)

'O Love, how thou art tired out with rhyme!'

O Love, how thou art tired out with rhyme!
Thou art a tree whereon all poets climb;
And from thy branches every one takes some
Of thy sweet fruit, which Fancy feeds upon.
But now thy tree is left so bare and poor,
That they can scarcely gather one plum more.

LEO MARKS (1921–2001)

The Life That I Have

The life that I have
Is all that I have
And the life that I have
Is yours.

The love that I have
Of the life that I have
Is yours and yours and yours.

A sleep I shall have
A rest I shall have,
Yet death will be but a pause,

For the peace of my years
In the long green grass
Will be yours and yours and yours.

CHRISTOPHER MARLOWE (1564–1593)

from **Hero and Leander**

It lies not in our power to love, or hate,
For will in us is overruled by fate.
When two are stripped, long ere the course begin
We wish that one should lose, the other win;
And one especially do we affect,
Of two gold ingots like in each respect.
The reason no man knows, let it suffice,
What we behold is censured by our eyes.
Where both deliberate, the love is slight;
Who ever loved, that loved not at first sight?

The Passionate Shepherd to His Love

Come live with me and be my Love,
And we will all the pleasures prove
That hills and valleys, dale and field,
And all the craggy mountains yield.

There will we sit upon the rocks
And see the shepherds feed their flocks,
By shallow rivers, to whose falls
Melodious birds sing madrigals.

There will I make thee beds of roses
And a thousand fragrant posies,
A cap of flowers, and a kirtle
Embroider'd all with leaves of myrtle.

A gown made of the finest wool
Which from our pretty lambs we pull,
Fair linèd slippers for the cold,
With buckles of the purest gold.

A belt of straw and ivy buds
With coral clasps and amber studs:
And if these pleasures may thee move,
Come live with me and be my Love.

Thy silver dishes for thy meat
As precious as the gods do eat,
Shall on an ivory table be
Prepared each day for thee and me.

The shepherd swains shall dance and sing
For thy delight each May morning:
If these delights thy mind may move,
Then live with me and be my Love.

DON MARQUIS (1878–1937)

from **The Song of Mehitabel**

i know that i am bound
for a journey down the sound
in the midst of a refuse mound
but wotthehell wotthehell
oh i should worry and fret
death and i will coquette
there's a dance in the old dame yet
toujours gai toujours gai

i once was an innocent kit
wotthehell wotthehell
with a ribbon my neck to fit
and bells tied onto it
o wotthehell wotthehell
but a maltese cat came by
with a come hither look in his eye
and a song that soared to the sky
and wotthehell wotthehell

and i followed adown the street
the pad of his rhythmical feet
o permit me again to repeat
wotthehell wotthehell
my youth i shall never forget
but there s nothing i really regret
wotthehell wotthehell
there s a dance in the old dame yet
toujours gai toujours gai

ANDREW MARVELL (1621–1678)

To His Coy Mistress

Had we but world enough, and time.
This coyness, lady, were no crime.
We would sit down, and think which way
To walk, and pass our long love's day.
Thou by the Indian Ganges' side
Should'st rubies find: I by the tide
Of Humber would complain. I would
Love you ten years before the Flood,
And you should, if you please, refuse
Till the conversion of the Jews.
My vegetable love should grow
Vaster than empires, and more slow.
An hundred years should go to praise
Thine eyes, and on thy forehead gaze:
Two hundred to adore each breast;
But thirty thousand to the rest;
An age at least to every part,
And the last age should show your heart.
For, lady, you deserve this state,

Nor would I love at lower rate.
    But at my back I always hear
Time's wingèd chariot hurrying near:
And yonder all before us lie
Deserts of vast eternity.
Thy beauty shall no more be found;
Nor, in thy marble vault, shall sound
My echoing song: then worms shall try
That long-preserved virginity,
And your quaint honour turn to dust,
And into ashes all my lust.
The grave's a fine and private place,
But none, I think, do there embrace.
    Now, therefore, while the youthful hue
Sits on thy skin like morning dew,
And while thy willing soul transpires
At every pore with instant fires,
Now let us sport us while we may;
And now, like amorous birds of prey,
Rather at once our Time devour,
Than languish in his slow-chapt power.
Let us roll all our strength and all
Our sweetness up into one ball,

And tear our pleasures with rough strife
Thorough the iron gates of life.
Thus, though we cannot make our Sun
Stand still, yet we will make him run.

CHARLOTTE MEW (1869–1928)

Sea Love

Tide be runnin' the great world over:
    'Twas only last June month I mind that we
Was thinkin' the toss and the call in the breast of
    the lover
    So everlastin' as the sea.

Here's the same little fishes that sputter and swim,
    Wi' the moon's old glim on the gray, wet sand;
An' him no more to me nor me to him
    Than the wind goin' over my hand.

A Quoi Bon Dire

Seventeen years ago you said
    Something that sounded like Good-bye:
And everybody thinks you are dead
    But I.

So I, as I grow stiff and cold
    To this and that say Good-bye too;
And everybody sees that I am old
        But you.

And one fine morning in a sunny lane
    Some boy and girl will meet and kiss and swear
        That nobody can love their way again
While over there
    You will have smiled, and I shall have tossed
        your hair.

The Peddler

Lend me, a little while, the key
    That locks your heavy heart, and I'll give you back—
Rarer than books and ribbons and beads bright to see,
    This little Key of Dreams out of my pack.

The road, the road, beyond men's bolted doors,
    There shall I walk and you go free of me,

For yours lies North across the moors,
    And mine lies South. To what seas?

How if we stopped and let our solemn selves go by,
    While my gay ghost caught and kissed yours, as
        ghosts don't do,
And by the wayside, this forgotten you and I
    Sat, and were twenty-two?

Give me the key that locks your tired eyes,
    And I will lend you this one from my pack,
Brighter than colored beads and painted books that
    make men wise:
    Take it. No, give it back!

I so liked Spring

I so liked Spring last year
    Because you were here; –
        The thrushes too –
Because it was these you so liked to hear –
        I so liked you.

This year's a different thing, –
    I'll not think of you.
But I'll like Spring because it is simply Spring
    As the thrushes do.

EDNA ST VINCENT MILLAY (1892–1950)

'love is not all'

Love is not all: It is not meat nor drink
Nor slumber nor a roof against the rain,
Nor yet a floating spar to men that sink
and rise and sink and rise and sink again.
Love cannot fill the thickened lung with breath
Nor clean the blood, nor set the fractured bone;
Yet many a man is making friends with death
even as I speak, for lack of love alone.
It well may be that in a difficult hour,
pinned down by need and moaning for release
or nagged by want past resolutions power,
I might be driven to sell your love for peace,
Or trade the memory of this night for food.
It may well be. I do not think I would.

JOHN MILTON (1608–1674)

'Methought I saw my late espoused Saint'

Methought I saw my late espoused Saint
Brought to me like Alcestis from the grave,
Whom Jove's great Son to her glad Husband gave,
Rescued from death by force though pale and faint.
Mine as whom washt from spot of child-bed taint,
Purification in the old Law did save,
And such, as yet once more I trust to have
Full sight of her in Heaven without restraint,
Came vested all in white, pure as her mind:
Her face was veiled, yet to my fancied sight,
Love, sweetness, goodness, in her person shined
So clear, as in no face with more delight.
But O as to embrace me she enclined
I waked, she fled, and day brought back my night.

ADRIAN MITCHELL (born 1932)

Celia, Celia

When I am sad and weary
When I think all hope has gone
When I walk along High Holborn
I think of you with nothing on.

LADY MARY WORTLEY MONTAGU
(1689–1762)

A Receipt to Cure the Vapours

Why will Delia thus retire,
And idly languish life away?
While the sighing crowd admire,
'Tis too soon for hartshorn tea.

All those dismal looks and fretting
Cannot Damon's life restore;
Long ago the worms have ate him,
You can never see him more.

Once again consult your toilet,
In the glass your face review:
So much weeping soon will spoil it,
And no spring your charms renew.

I, like you, was born a woman,
Well I know what vapours mean:

The disease, alas! is common;
Single, we have all the spleen.

All the morals that they tell us
Never cured the sorrow yet:
Choose, among the pretty fellows,
One of humour, youth and wit.

Prithee hear him every morning,
At the least an hour or two;
Once again at night returning
I believe the dose will do.

THOMAS MOORE (1779–1852)

At the Mid Hour of Night

At the mid hour of night, when stars are weeping, I fly
To the lone vale we loved, when life shone warm in
thine eye;
And I think oft, if spirits can steal from the regions of
air
To revisit past scenes of delight, thou wilt come to
me there,
And tell me our love is remembered even in the sky.

Then I sing the wild song it once was rapture to hear,
When our voices commingling breathed like one on
the ear;
And as Echo far off through the vale my sad orison
rolls,
I think, O my love! 'tis thy voice from the Kingdom of
Souls
Faintly answering still the notes that once were so
dear.

'Believe me, if all those endearing young charms'

Believe me, if all those endearing young charms
Which I gaze on so fondly to-day,
Were to change by to-morrow and fleet in my arms,
Like fairy gifts fading away.
Thou wouldst still be adored as this moment thou art,
Let thy loveliness fade as it will,
And around the dear ruin each wish of my heart,
Would entwine itself verdantly still.

It is not while beauty and youth are thine own
And thy cheeks unprofaned by a tear,
That the fervor and faith of a soul can be known,
To which time will but make thee more dear:
No, the heart that has truly loved never forgets,
But as truly loves on to the close,
As the sun-flower turns on her god when he sets
The same look which she turned when he rose.

Love's Young Dream

Oh! the days are gone, when Beauty bright
My heart's chain wove;
When my dream of life, from morn till night,
Was love, still love.
New hope may bloom,
And days may come,
Of milder calmer beam,
But there's nothing half so sweet in life
As love's young dream:
No, there's nothing half so sweet in life
As love's young dream.

Though the bard to purer fame may soar,
When wild youth's past;
Though he win the wise, who frowned before,
To smile at last;
He'll never meet
A joy so sweet,
In all his noon of fame,
As when first he sung to woman's ear
His soul-felt flame,

And, at every close, she blushed to hear
The one loved name.

No, – that hallowed form is ne'er forgot
Which first love traced;
Still it lingering haunts the greenest spot
On memory's waste.
'Twas odour fled
As soon as shed;
'Twas morning's winged dream;
'Twas a light, that ne'er can shine again
On life's dull stream:
Oh! 'twas light that n'er can shine again
On life's dull stream.

EDWIN MORGAN (born 1920)

One Cigarette

No smoke without you, my fire.
After you left,
your cigarette glowed on in my ashtray
and sent up a long thread of such quiet grey
I smiled to wonder who would believe its signal
of so much love. One cigarette
in the non-smoker's tray.
As the last spire
trembles up, a sudden draught
blows it winding into my face.
Is it smell, is it taste?
You are here again, and I am drunk on your tobacco
    lips.
Out with the light.
Let the smoke lie back in the dark.
Till I hear the very ash
sigh down among the flowers of brass
I'll breathe, and long past midnight, your last kiss.

WILLIAM MORRIS (1834–1896)

from **Love is Enough**

Love is enough: though the World be a-waning,
And the woods have no voice but the voice of
 complaining,
Though the sky be too dark for dim eyes to discover
The gold-cups and daisies fair blooming thereunder,
Though the hills be held shadows, and the sea a dark
 wonder,
And this day draw a veil over all deeds passed over,
Yet their hands shall not tremble, their feet shall not
 falter;
The void shall not weary, the fear shall not alter
These lips and these eyes of the loved and the lover.

EDWIN MUIR (1887–1959)

The Confirmation

Yes yours, my love, is the right human face.
I in my mind had waited for this long,
Seeing the false and searching for the true,
Then found you as a traveller finds a place
Of welcome suddenly amid the wrong
Valleys and rocks and twisting roads. But you,
What shall I call you? A fountain in a waste,
A well of water in a country dry,
Or anything that's honest and good, an eye
That makes the whole world bright. Your open heart,
Simple with giving, gives the primal deed,
The first good world, the blossom, the blowing seed,
The hearth, the steadfast land, the wandering sea,
Not beautiful and rare in every part.
But like yourself, as they were meant to be.

JOHN FREDERICK NIMS (1913–1999)

Love Poem

My clumsiest dear, whose hands shipwreck vases,
At whose quick touch all glasses chip and ring,
Whose palms are bulls in china, burrs in linen
And have no cunning with any soft thing

Except at ill-at-ease fidgeting people:
The refugee uncertain at the door
You make a steady home; deftly you steady
The drunk clambering on his undulant floor

Unpredictable dear, the taxi driver's terror,
Shrinking from far headlights pale as a dime
Yet leaping before red apoplectic streetcars –
Misfit in any space. And never on time.

A wrench in clocks and the solar system. Only
With words and people and love you move at ease.
In traffic of wit expertly manoeuvre
And keep us, all devotion, at your knees.

Forgetting your coffee spreading on our flannel,
Your lipstick grinning on our coat,
So gaily in love's unbreakable heaven
Our souls on glory of spilt bourbon float.

Be with me, darling, early and late. Smash glasses –
I will study wry music for your sake.
For should your hands drop white and empty
All the toys of the world would break.

CAROLINE NORTON (1808–1877)

'We have been friends together'

We have been friends together
    In sunshine and in shade,
Since first beneath the chestnut trees,
    In infancy we played.

But coldness dwells within thy heart,
    A cloud is on thy brow;
We have been friends together,
    Shall a light word part us now?

We have been gay together;
    We have laughed at little jests;
For the fount of hope was gushing
    Warm and joyous in our breasts,

But laughter now hath fled thy lip,
    And sullen glooms thy brow;
We have been gay together,
    Shall a light word part us now?

We have been sad together;
    We have wept with bitter tears
O'er the grass-grown graves where slumbered
    The hopes of early years.

The voices which are silent there
    Would bid thee clear thy brow;
We have been sad together.
    Oh, what shall part us now?

DOROTHY PARKER (1893–1967)

Theory

Into love and out again,
 Thus I went, and thus I go.
Spare your voice, and hold your pen –
 Well and bitterly I know
All the songs were ever sung,
 All the words were ever said;
Could it be, when I was young,
 Some one dropped me on my head?

Comment

Oh, life is a glorious cycle of song,
A medley of extemporanea;
And love is a thing that can never go wrong;
And I am Marie of Roumania.

ANNA PARNELL (1852–1911)

'Two children playing by a stream'

Two children playing by a stream
Two lovers walking in a dream
A married pair whose dream is o'er
Two old folks who are quite a bore.

BRIAN PATTEN (born 1946)

'Into my mirror has walked'

Into my mirror has walked
A woman who will not talk
Of love or of its subsidiaries,
But who stands there,
Pleased by her own silence.
The weather has worn into her
All seasons known to me,
In one breast she holds
Evidence of forests,
In the other, of seas.

I will ask her nothing yet
Would ask so much
If she gave some sign –

Her shape is common enough,
Enough shape to love.
But what keeps me here
Is what glows beyond her.

I think at times
A boy's body
Would be as easy
To read light into,
I think at times
My own might do.

GEORGE PEELE (1556–1596)

Bethsabe's Song

Hot sun, cool fire, tempered with sweet air,
Black shade, fair nurse, shadow my white hair;
Shine, sun; burn, fire; breathe, air, and ease me;
Black shade, fair nurse, shroud me and please me:
Shadow, my sweet nurse, keep me from burning,
Make not my glad cause cause of mourning.

    Let not my beauty's fire
    Inflame unstaid desire,
    Nor pierce any bright eye
    That wandereth lightly.

from **The Hunting of Cupid**

What thing is love? (for well I wot) love is a thing.
It is a prick, it is a sting,
It is a pretty pretty thing;
It is a fire, it is a coal,
Whose flame creeps in at every hole;

And as my wit doth best devise,
Love's dwelling is in ladies' eyes:
From whence do glance love's piercing darts
That make such holes into our hearts;
And all the world herein accord
Love is a great and mighty lord,

And when he list to mount so high,
With Venus he in heaven doth lie,
And evermore hath been a god
Since Mars and she played even and odd.

KATHERINE PHILIPS (1632–1664)

To my Excellent Lucasia, on our Friendship

I did not live until this time
    Crowned my felicity,
When I could say without a crime,
    I am not thine, but Thee.

This Carcass breathed, and walked, and slept,
    So that the World believed
There was a Soul the Motions kept;
    But they were all deceived.

For as a Watch by art is wound
    To motion, such was mine:
But never had Orinda found
    A Soul till she found thine;

Which now inspires, cures and supplies,
    And guides my darkened Breast:
For thou art all that I can prize,
    My Joy, my Life, my Rest.

No Bridegrooms nor Crown-conquerors mirth
    To mine compared can be:
They have but pieces of this Earth,
    I've all the World in thee.

Then let our Flames still light and shine,
    And no false fear control,
As innocent as our Design,
    Immortal as our Soul.

EDGAR ALLAN POE (1809–1849)

To Helen

Helen, thy beauty is to me
   Like those Nicean barks of yore,
That gently, o'er a perfumed sea,
   The weary, wayworn wanderer bore
   To his own native shore.

On desperate seas long wont to roam,
   Thy hyacinth hair, thy classic face,
Thy Naiad airs have brought me home
   To the glory that was Greece
And the grandeur that was Rome.

Lo! in yon brilliant window-niche
   How statue-like I see thee stand,
   The agate lamp within thy hand!
Ah, Psyche, from the regions which
   Are Holy Land!

To One in Paradise

Thou wast all that to me, love,
   For which my soul did pine:
A green isle in the sea, love,
   A fountain and a shrine
All wreathed with fairy fruits and flowers,
   And all the flowers were mine.

Ah, dream too bright to last!
   Ah, starry Hope, that didst arise
But to be overcast!
   A voice from out the Future cries,
'On! on!' – but o'er the Past
   (Dim gulf!) my spirit hovering lies
Mute, motionless, aghast.

For, alas! alas! with me
   The light of Life is o'er!
No more – no more – no more –
(Such language holds the solemn sea
   To the sands upon the shore)

Shall bloom the thunder-blasted tree,
    Or the stricken eagle soar.

And all my days are trances,
    And all my nightly dreams
Are where thy grey eye glances,
    And where thy footstep gleams –
In what ethereal dances,
    By what eternal streams.

SIR WALTER RALEIGH (c.1552–1618)

'As you came from the holy land'

As you came from the holy land
Of Walsinghame
Met you not with my true love
By the way as you came?

How shall I know your true love,
That have met many one,
As I went to the holy land,
That have come, that have gone?

She is neither white nor brown,
But as the heavens fair;
There is none hath a form so divine
In the earth or the air.

Such a one did I meet, good sir,
Such an angel-like face,
Who like a queen, like a nymph, did appear,
By her gait, by her grace.

She hath left me here all alone,
All alone, as unknown,
Who sometimes did me lead with herself,
And me loved as her own.

What's the cause that she leaves you alone,
And a new way doth take,
Who loved you once as her own,
And her joy did you make?

I have loved her all my youth,
But now old, as you see,
Love likes not the falling fruit
From the withered tree:

Know that love is a careless child,
And forgets promise past;
He is blind, he is deaf when he list,
And in faith never fast.

His desire is a dureless content,
And a trustless joy;
He is won with a world of despair,
And is lost with a toy:

Of womankind such indeed is the love
Or the word love abusèd,
Under which many childish desires
And conceits are excusèd.

But true love is a durable fire,
In the mind ever burning,
Never sick, never old, never dead,
From itself never turning.

The Nymph's Reply to the Shepherd

If all the world and love were young,
And truth in every shepherd's tongue,
These pretty pleasures might me move,
To live with thee and be thy love.

Time drives the flocks from field to fold,
When rivers rage, and rocks grow cold;
And Philomel becometh dumb;
The rest complains of cares to come.

The flowers do fade, and wanton fields
To wayward winter reckoning yields;
A honey tongue, a heart of gall,
Is fancy's spring, but sorrow's fall.

They gowns, thy shoes, thy beds of roses,
Thy cap, thy kirtle, and thy posies,
Soon break, soon wither, soon forgotten;
In folly ripe, in reason rotten.

Thy belt of straw and ivy buds,
Thy coral clasps and amber studs,
All these in me no means can move,
To come to thee and be thy love.

But could youth last, and love still breed,
Had joys no date, nor age no need,
Then these delights my mind might move
To live with thee and be thy love.

ALLAN RAMSAY (1686–1758)

Sang

My Peggy is a young thing,
   Just enter'd in her teens,
Fair as the day, and sweet as May,
Fair as the day, and always gay;
   My Peggy is a young thing,
   And I'm not very auld,
Yet well I like to meet her at
   The wawking of the fauld[1].

My Peggy speaks sae sweetly
   Whene'er we meet alane,
I wish nae mair to lay my care,
I wish nae mair of a' that's rare;
   My Peggy speaks sae sweetly,
   To a' the lave[2] I'm cauld,
But she gars[3] a' my spirits glow
   At wawking of the fauld.

My Peggy smiles sae kindly
    Whene'er I whisper love,
That I look down on a' the town,
That I look down upon a crown;
    My Peggy smiles sae kindly,
    It makes me blyth and bauld,
And naething gi'es me sic delight
    As wawking of the fauld.

My Peggy sings sae saftly
    When on my pipe I play,
By a' the rest it is confest,
By a' the rest, that she sings best;
    My Peggy sings sae saftly,
    And in her sangs are tauld,
With innocence the wale[4] of sense,
    At wawking of the fauld.

[1] wawking of the fauld = watching over the sheepfold.
[2] lave = rest. [3] gars = makes. [4] wale = choice.

HENRY REED (1914–1986)

Judging Distances (II)
(from 'Lessons of the War')

Not only how far away, but the way that you say it
Is very important. Perhaps you may never get
The knack of judging a distance, but at least you know
How to report on a landscape: the central sector,
The right of arc and that, which we had last Tuesday,
    And at least you know

That maps are of time, not place, so far as the army
Happens to be concerned – the reason being,
Is one which need not delay us. Again, you know
There are three kinds of tree, three only, the fir and
    the poplar,
And those which have bushy tops to; and lastly
    That things only seem to be things.

A barn is not called a barn, to put it more plainly,
Or a field in the distance, where sheep may be safely
    grazing.

You must never be over-sure. You must say, when
    reporting:
At five o'clock in the central sector is a dozen
Of what appear to be animals; whatever you do,
    Don't call the bleeders sheep.

I am sure that's quite clear; and suppose, for the sake
    of example,
The one at the end, asleep, endeavours to tell us
What he sees over there to the west, and how far away,
After first having come to attention. There to the west,
On the fields of summer the sun and the shadows
    bestow
    Vestments of purple and gold.

The white dwellings are like a mirage in the heat,
And under the swaying elms a man and a woman
Lie gently together. Which is, perhaps, only to say
That there is a row of houses to the left of arc,
And that under some poplars a pair of what appear
    to be humans
    Appear to be loving.

Well that, for an answer, is what we rightly call
Moderately satisfactory only, the reason being,
Is that two things have been omitted, and those are
    very important.
The human beings, now: in what direction are they,
And how far away, would you say? And do not forget
    There may be dead ground in between.

There may be dead ground in between; and I may
    not have got
The knack of judging a distance; I will only venture
A guess that perhaps between me and the apparent
    lovers,
(Who, incidentally, appear by now to have finished)
At seven o'clock from the houses, is roughly a
    distance
    Of about one year and a half.

CHRISTINA GEORGINA ROSSETTI
(1830–1894)

'Remember'

Remember me when I am gone away,
Gone far away into the silent land;
When you can no more hold me by the hand,
Nor I half turn to go, yet turning stay.
Remember me when no more, day by day,
You tell me of our future that you planned;
Only remember me; you understand
It will be late to counsel then or pray.
Yet if you should forget me for a while
And afterwards remember, do not grieve;
For if the darkness and corruption leave
A vestige of the thoughts that once I had,
Better by far you should forget and smile
Than that you should remember and be sad.

A Birthday

My heart is like a singing bird
   Whose nest is in a watered shoot;
My heart is like an apple-tree
   Whose boughs are bent with thickset fruit;
My heart is like a rainbow shell
   That paddles in a halcyon sea;
My heart is gladder than all these
   Because my love is come to me.

Raise me a dais of silk and down;
   Hang it with vair and purple dyes;
Carve it in doves and pomegranates,
   And peacocks with a hundred eyes;
Work it in gold and silver grapes,
   In leaves and silver fleurs-de-lys;
Because the birthday of my life
   Is come, my love is come to me.

Echo

Come to me in the silence of the night;
    Come in the speaking silence of a dream;
Come with soft rounded cheeks and eyes as
      bright
    As sunlight on a stream;
    Come back in tears,
O memory, hope and love of finished years.

O dream how sweet, too sweet, too bitter-sweet,
    Whose wakening should have been in Paradise,
Where souls brim-full of love abide and meet;
    Where thirsting longing eyes
    Watch the slow door
That opening, letting in, lets out no more.

Yet come to me in dreams, that I may live
    My very life again though cold in death;
Come back to me in dreams, that I may give
    Pulse for pulse, breath for breath:
    Speak low, lean low,
As long ago, my love, how long ago.

Promises Like Pie-crust

Promise me no promises,
So will I not promise you:
Keep we both our liberties,
Never false and never true:
Let us hold the die uncast,
Free to come as free to go:
For I cannot know your past,
And of mine what can you know?

You, so warm, may once have been
Warmer towards another one:
I, so cold, may once have seen
Sunlight, once have felt the sun:
Who shall show us if it was
Thus indeed in time of old?
Fades the image from the glass,
And the fortune is not told.

If you promised, you might grieve
For lost liberty again:
If I promised, I believe

I should fret to break the chain.
Let us be the friends we were,
Nothing more but nothing less:
Many thrive on frugal fare
Who would perish of excess.

'I loved you first'

(from 'Monna Innominata')

'Poca favilla gran fiamma seconda.' – Dante

*'Ogni altra cosa, ogni pensier va fore,
E sol ivi con voi rimansi amore.'* – Petrarch

I loved you first: but afterwards your love
Outsoaring mine, sang such a loftier song
As drowned the friendly cooings of my dove.
Which owes the other most? my love was long,
And yours one moment seemed to wax more strong;
I loved and guessed at you, you construed me

And loved me for what might or might not be-
Nay, weights and measures do us both a wrong.
For verily love knows not 'mine' or 'thine;'
With separate 'I' and 'thou' free love has done,
For one is both and both are one in love:
Rich love knows nought of 'thine that is not mine;'
Both have the strength and both the length thereof,
Both of us, of the love which makes us one.

DANTE GABRIEL ROSSETTI (1830–1894)

Silent Noon

Your hands lie open in the long fresh grass,–
The finger-points look through like rosy blooms:
Your eyes smile peace. The pasture gleams and
    glooms
'Neath billowing skies that scatter and amass.
All round our nest, far as the eye can pass,
Are golden kingcup-fields with silver edge
Where the cow-parsley skirts the hawthorn-hedge.
'Tis visible silence, still as the hour-glass.

Deep in the sun-searched growths the dragon-fly
Hangs like a blue thread loosen'd from the sky:–
So this winged hour is dropt to us from above.
Oh! clasp we to our hearts, for deathless dower,
This close-companioned inarticulate hour
When twofold silence was the song of love.

Sudden Light

I have been here before,
But when or how I cannot tell:
I know the grass beyond the door,
The sweet keen smell,
The sighing sound, the lights around the shore.

You have been mine before,–
How long ago I may not know:
But just when at that swallow's soar
Your neck turned so,
Some veil did fall, – I knew it all of yore.

Has this been thus before?
And shall not thus time's eddying flight
Still with our lives our love restore
In death's despite,
And day and night yield one delight once more?

Severed Selves

Two separate divided silences,
Which, brought together, would find loving voice;
Two glances which together would rejoice
In love, now lost like stars beyond dark trees;
Two hands apart whose touch alone gives ease;
Two bosoms which, heart-shrined with mutual
    flame,
Would, meeting in one clasp, be made the same;
Two souls, the shores wave-mocked of sundering
    seas:–
Such are we now. Ah! may our hope forecast
Indeed one hour again, when on this stream
Of darkened love once more the light shall gleam? –
An hour how slow to come, how quickly past, –
Which blooms and fades, and only leaves at last,
Faint as shed flowers, the attenuated dream.

SAPPHO (fl. 7th–6th century BC)

The moon sinks, and the Pleiades:
Midnight is come, the watchman passes,
And I lie here alone.

SIR WALTER SCOTT (1771–1832)

from **Woodstock**

An hour with thee! When earliest day
Dapples with gold the eastern grey,
Oh, what can frame my mind to bear
The toil and turmoil, cark[1] and care,
New griefs, which coming hours unfold,
And sad remembrance of the old?
One hour with thee.

One hour with thee! When burning June
Waves his red flag at pitch of noon;
What shall repay the faithful swain,
His labour on the sultry plain;
And, more than cave or sheltering bough,
Cool feverish blood and throbbing brow?
One hour with thee.

[1] cark = worry.

One hour with thee! When sun is set,
Oh, what can teach me to forget
The thankless labours of the day;
The hopes, the wishes, flung away;
The increasing wants, and lessening gains,
The master's pride, who scorns my pains?
One hour with thee.

SIR CHARLES SEDLEY (c.1639–1701)

'Love still has something of the Sea'

Love still has something of the Sea,
From whence his Mother rose;
No time his slaves from doubt can free,
Nor give their thoughts repose.

They are becalmed in clearest days,
And in rough weather tossed;
They wither under cold delays,
Or are in tempests lost.

One while they seem to touch the port,
Then straight into the main
Some angry wind in cruel sport
Their vessel drives again.

At first disdain and pride they fear,
Which, if they chance to 'scape,
Rivals and falsehood soon appear
In a more dreadful shape.

By such degrees to joy they come,
And are so long withstood,
So slowly they receive the sum,
It hardly does them good.

'Tis cruel to prolong a pain;
And to defer a joy,
Believe me, gentle Celemene,
Offends the winged boy.

An hundred thousand oaths your fears
Perhaps would not remove,
And if I gazed a thousand years,
I could no deeper love.

WILLIAM SHAKESPEARE (1564–1616)

'Who is Sylvia?'
(from 'Two Gentlemen of Verona', Act 4, Scene 2)

Who is Sylvia? What is she,
    That all our swains commend her?
Holy, fair, and wise is she;
    The heaven such grace did lend her
That she might admirèd be.

Is she kind, as she is fair?
    For beauty lives with kindness.
Love doth to her eyes repair,
    To help him of his blindness;
And, being helped, inhabits there.

Then to Sylvia let us sing,
    That Sylvia is excelling;
She excels each mortal thing
    Upon the dull earth dwelling;
To her let us garlands bring.

content

body

'It was a lover and his lass'
(from 'As You Like It', Act 5, Scene 3)

It was a lover and his lass
    With a hey, and a ho, and a hey nonino,
That o'er the green cornfield did pass
    In the spring-time, the only pretty ring-time,
When birds do sing, hey ding a ding, ding;
    Sweet lovers love the spring.

Between the acres of the rye
    With a hey, and a ho, and a hey nonino,
These pretty country folks would lie,
    In the spring-time, the only pretty ring-time,
When birds do sing, hey ding a ding, ding;
    Sweet lovers love the spring.

This carol they began that hour,
    With a hey, and a ho, and a hey nonino,
How that life was but a flower
    In the spring-time, the only pretty ring-time,
When birds do sing, hey ding a ding, ding;
    Sweet lovers love the spring.

And therefore take the present time
    With a hey, and a ho, and a hey nonino,
For love is crownèd with the prime
In the spring-time, the only pretty ring-time,
When birds do sing, hey ding a ding, ding;
    Sweet lovers love the spring.

'If music be the food of love'
(from 'Twelfth Night', Act 1, Scene 1)

If music be the food of love, play on;
Give me excess of it, that, surfeiting,
The appetite may sicken, and so die.
That strain again! it had a dying fall:
O, it came o'er my ear like the sweet sound,
That breathes upon a bank of violets,
Stealing and giving odour! Enough; no more:
'Tis not so sweet now as it was before.
O spirit of love, how quick and fresh art thou,
That, notwithstanding thy capacity
Receiveth as the sea, nought enters there,
Of what validity and pitch soe'er,
But falls into abatement and low price,
Even in a minute: so full of shapes is fancy
That it alone is high fantastical.

'O Mistress mine'
(from 'Twelfth Night', Act 2, Scene 3)

O Mistress mine, where are you roaming?
O stay and hear! your true love's coming
   That can sing both high and low;
Trip no further, pretty sweeting,
Journeys end in lovers meeting –
   Every wise man's son doth know.

What is love? 'tis not hereafter;
Present mirth hath present laughter;
   What's to come is still unsure:
In delay there lies no plenty, –
Then come kiss me, sweet-and-twenty,
   Youth's a stuff will not endure.

'Take, O take those lips away'
(from 'Measure for Measure', Act 4, Scene 1)

Take, O take those lips away
    That so sweetly were forsworn,
And those eyes, the break of day,
    Lights that do mislead the morn.
But my kisses bring again, bring again –
Seals of love, but sealed in vain, sealed in vain!

(from 'Romeo and Juliet', Act 2, Scene 2)

My bounty is as boundless as the sea,
My love as deep; the more I give to thee,
The more I have, for both are infinite.

(from 'The Merchant of Venice', Act 3, Scene 2)

One half of me is yours, the other half yours –
Mine own, I would say; but if mine, then yours,
And so all yours.

(from 'Love's Labour's Lost', Act 4, Scene 3)

A lover's eyes will gaze an eagle blind;
A lover's ear will hear the lowest sound,
When the suspicious head of theft is stopped:
Love's feeling is more soft and sensible
Than are the tender horns of cockled snails;
Love's tongue proves dainty Bacchus gross in taste:
For valour, is not Love a Hercules,
Still climbing trees in the Hesperides?
Subtle as Sphinx; as sweet and musical
As bright Apollo's lute, strung with his hair:
And when Love speaks, the voice of all the gods
Makes heaven drowsy with the harmony.
Never durst poet touch a pen to write
Until his ink were tempered with Love's sighs;
O, then his lines would ravish savage ears
And plant in tyrants mild humility.
From women's eyes this doctrine I derive:
They sparkle still the right Promethean fire;
They are the books, the arts, the academes,
That show, contain and nourish all the world:
Else none at all in ought proves excellent.

(from 'The Winter's Tale', Act 4 Scene 4)

What you do
Still betters what is done. When you speak, sweet,
I'd have you do it ever; when you sing,
I'd have you buy and sell so; so give alms;
Pray so; and for the ord'ring your affairs,
To sing them too. When you do dance, I wish you
A wave o' th' sea, that you might ever do
Nothing but that; move still, still so,
And own no other function. Each your doing,
So singular in each particular,
Crowns what you are doing in the present deeds,
That all your acts are queens.

(from 'Twelfth Night', Act 3, Scene 1)

I love thee so that, maugre all thy pride,
Nor wit nor reason can my passion hide.
Do not extort thy reasons from this clause,
For that I woo, thou therefore hast no cause;
But rather reason thus with reason fetter,
Love sought is good, but given unsought better.

Sonnet 18

Shall I compare thee to a summer's day?
Thou art more lovely and more temperate;
Rough winds do shake the darling buds of May,
And summer's lease hath all too short a date:
Sometime too hot the eye of heaven shines,
And often is his gold complexion dimmed:
And every fair from fair sometime declines,
By chance, or nature's changing course untrimmed:
But thy eternal summer shall not fade
Nor lose possession of that fair thou owest;
Nor shall Death brag thou wanderest in his shade
When in eternal lines to time thou growest.
    So long as men can breathe, or eyes can see,
    So long lives this, and this gives life to thee.

Sonnet 29

When in disgrace with Fortune and men's eyes
I all alone beweep my outcast state,
And trouble deaf heaven with my bootless cries,
And look upon myself, and curse my fate,

Wishing me like to one more rich in hope,
Featured like him, like him with friends possessed,
Desiring this man's art, and that man's scope,
With what I most enjoy contented least;
Yet in these thoughts myself almost despising,
Haply I think on thee, and then my state,
Like to the lark at break of day arising
From sullen earth, sings hymns at heaven's gate;
    For thy sweet love remembered such wealth
    brings
      That then I scorn to change my state with kings.

Sonnet 43

When most I wink then do mine eyes best see,
For all the day they view things unrespected,
But when I sleep, in dreams they look on thee,
And darkly bright, are bright in dark directed.
Then thou whose shadow shadows doth make bright
How would thy shadow's form, form happy show,
To the clear day with thy much clearer light,
When to unseeing eyes thy shade shines so!
How would, I say, mine eyes be blessèd made,

By looking on thee in the living day,
When in dead night thy fair imperfect shade,
Through heavy sleep on sightless eyes doth stay!
    All days are nights to see till I see thee,
    And nights bright days when dreams do show
    thee me.

Sonnet 104

To me, fair friend, you never can be old,
For as you were when first your eye I eyed,
Such seems your beauty still. Three winters cold,
Have from the forests shook three summers' pride,
Three beauteous springs to yellow autumn turned,
In process of the seasons have I seen,
Three April perfumes in three hot Junes burned,
Since first I saw you fresh which yet are green.
Ah, yet doth beauty like a dial hand,
Steal from his figure, and no pace perceived,
So your sweet hue, which methinks still doth stand
Hath motion, and mine eye may be deceived.
    For fear of which, hear this thou age unbred:
    Ere you were born was beauty's summer dead.

Sonnet 116

Let me not to the marriage of true minds
Admit impediments: Love is not love
Which alters when it alteration finds,
Or bends with the remover to remove.
O no, it is an ever-fixèd mark
That looks on tempests and is never shaken;
It is the star to every wandering bark,
Whose worth's unknown, although his height be
    taken.
Love's not Time's fool, though rosy lips and cheeks
Within his bending sickle's compass come;
Love alters not with his brief hours and weeks,
But bears it out even to the edge of doom.
    If this be error and upon me proved,
    I never writ, nor no man ever loved.

PERCY BYSSHE SHELLEY (1792–1822)

To —

Music, when soft voices die,
Vibrates in the memory –
Odours, when sweet violets sicken,
Live within the sense they quicken.

Rose leaves, when the rose is dead,
Are heaped for the belovèd's bed;
And so thy thoughts, when thou art gone,
Love itself shall slumber on.

'When the lamp is shattered'

When the lamp is shattered
The light in the dust lies dead
When the cloud is scattered
The rainbow's glory is shed.
When the lute is broken,

Sweet tones are remembered not.
　　When the lips have spoken,
Loved accents are soon forgot.

　　As music and splendour
Survive not the lamp and the lute.
　　The heart's echoes render
No song when the spirit is mute –
　　No song but sad dirges,
Like the wind through a ruined cell,
　　Or the mournful surges
That ring the dead seaman's knell.

　　When hearts have once mingled
Love first leaves the well-built nest.
　　The weak one is singled
To endure what it once possessed.
　　Oh Love! who bewailest
The frailty of all things here,
　　Why choose you the frailest
For your cradle, your home, and your bier?

Its passions will rock thee
As the storms rock the ravens on high.
    Bright reason will mock thee,
Like the sun from a wintry sky.
    From thy nest every rafter
Will rot, and thine eagle home
    Leave thee naked to laughter,
When leaves fall and cold winds come.

Love's Philosophy

The fountains mingle with the river,
And the rivers with the ocean,
The winds of heaven mix forever
With a sweet emotion;
Nothing in the world is single;
All things by law divine
In one another's being mingle; –
Why not I with thine?

See the mountains kiss high heaven
And the waves clasp one another
No sister flower would be forgiven
If it disdained its brother;
And sunlight clasps the earth,
And the moonbeams kiss the sea;
What are all these kissings worth
If thou kiss not me?

The Indian Serenade

I arise from dreams of thee
   In the first sweet sleep of night,
When the winds are breathing low,
   And the stars are shining bright.
I arise from dreams of thee,
   And a spirit in my feet
Hath led me-who knows how?
   To thy chamber window, Sweet!

The wandering airs they faint
   On the dark, the silent stream-
And the champak's[1] odours
   Like sweet thoughts in a dream;
The nightingale's complaint,
   It dies upon her heart,
As I must on thine,
   O belovèd as thou art!

O lift me from the grass!
   I die! I faint! I fail!
Let thy love in kisses rain
   On my lips and eyelids pale.
My cheek is cold and white, alas!
   My heart beats loud and fast:
O press it to thine own again,
   Where it will break at last!

---

[1] champak = Indian tree with fragrant flowers.

SIR PHILIP SIDNEY (1554–1586)

Sonnet

With how sad steps, O moon, thou climb'st the skies;
How silently and with how wan a face.
What! May it be that even in heav'nly place
That busy archer his sharp arrows tries?
Sure, if that long-with love acquainted eyes
Can judge of love, thou feel'st a lover's case;
I read it in thy looks, thy languished grace,
To me, that feel the like, thy state decries.
Then even of fellowship, O moon, tell me:
Is constant love deemed there but want of wit?
Are beauties there as proud as here they be?
Do they above love to be loved, and yet
Those lovers scorn whom that love doth possess?
Do they call virtue there ungratefulness?

'My true-love hath my heart'

My true-love hath my heart, and I have his,
By just exchange one to the other given:
I hold his dear, and mine he cannot miss,
There never was a better bargain driven:
My true-love hath my heart, and I have his.

His heart in me keeps him and me in one,
My heart in him his thoughts and senses guides:
He loves my heart, for once it was his own,
I cherish his because in me it bides:
My true-love hath my heart, and I have his.

WILLIAM SOUTAR (1898–1943)

The Tryst

O luely, luely cam she in,[1]
  And luely she lay doun:
I kent her by her caller lips[2]
  And her breists sae sma' and roun'.

A' thru the nicht we spak nae word
  Nor sinder'd bane frae bane:[3]
A' thru the nicht I heard her he'rt
  Gang soundin' wi' my ain.

It was about the waukrife hour[4]
  Whan cocks begin to craw
That she smool'd saftly thru the mirk[5]
  Afore the day wud daw.

Sae luely, luely, cam she in,
  Sae luely was she gaen;
And wi' her a' my simmer days
  Like they had never been.

[1] luely = quietly. [2] caller = cold. [3] sinder'd = sundered.
[4] waukrife = wakeful. [5] smool'd = slipped away; mirk = darkness.

EDMUND SPENSER (1552–1599)

Amoretti LXXV

One day I wrote her name upon the strand,
But came the waves and washed it away:
Again I wrote it with a second hand,
But came the tide, and made my pains his prey.
'Vain man,' said she, 'that dost in vain assay,
A mortal thing so to immortalize;
For I myself shall like to this decay,
And eke my name be wiped out likewise.'
'Not so,' (quod I) 'let baser things devise
To die in dust, but you shall live by fame:
My verse your vertues rare shall eternize,
And in the heavens write your glorious name:
Where whenas death shall all the world subdue,
Our love shall live, and later life renew.'

Ice and Fire

My love is like to ice, and I to fire:
How comes it then that this her cold so great
Is not dissolved through my so hot desire,
But harder grows the more I her entreat?
Or how comes it that my exceeding heat
Is not allayed by her heart-frozen cold,
But that I burn much more in boiling sweat,
And feel my flames augmented manifold?
What more miraculous thing may be told,
That fire, which all things melts, should harden ice,
And ice, which is congealed with senseless cold,
Should kindle fire by wonderful device?
Such is the power of love in gentle mind,
That it can alter all the course of kind.

ROBERT LOUIS STEVENSON
(1850–1894)

Romance

I will make you brooches and toys for your delight
Of bird-song at morning and star-shine at night,
I will make a palace fit for you and me
Of green days in forests, and blue days at sea.

I will make my kitchen, and you shall keep your room,
Where white flows the river and bright blows the
    broom;
And you shall wash your linen and keep your body
    white
In rainfall at morning and dewfall at night.

And this shall be for music when no one else is near,
The fine song for singing, the rare song to hear!
That only I remember, that only you admire,
Of the broad road that stretches and the roadside
    fire.

'Bright is the ring of words'

Bright is the ring of words
   When the right man rings them,
Fair the fall of songs
   When the singer sings them.
Still they are carolled and said –
   On wings they are carried –
After the singer is dead
   And the maker buried.

Low as the singer lies
   In the field of heather,
Songs of his fashion bring
   The swains together.
And when the west is red
   With the sunset embers,
The lover lingers and sings,
   And the maid remembers.

SIR JOHN SUCKLING (1609–1642)

A Constant Lover

Out upon it, I have loved
   Three whole days together!
And am like to love three more,
   If it prove fair weather.

Time shall moult away his wings
   Ere he shall discover
In the whole wide world again
   Such a constant lover.

But the spite on't is, no praise
   Is due at all to me:
Love with me had made no stays,
   Had it any been but she.

Had it any been but she,
   And that very face,
There had been at least ere this
   A dozen dozen in her place.

ALGERNON CHARLES SWINBURNE
(1837–1909)

Love and Sleep

Lying asleep between the strokes of night
I saw my love lean over my sad bed,
Pale as the duskiest lily's leaf or head,
Smooth-skinned and dark, with bare throat made to
    bite,
Too wan for blushing and too warm for white,
But perfect-coloured without white or red.
And her lips opened amorously, and said –
I wist not what, saving one word–Delight,
And all her face was honey to my mouth,
And all her body pasture to mine eyes;
The long lithe arms and hotter hands than fire,
The quivering flanks, hair smelling of the south,
The bright light feet, the splendid supple thighs
And glittering eyelids of my soul's desire.

ALFRED LORD TENNYSON (1809–1883)

Marriage Morning

Light, so low upon earth,
You send a flash to the sun.
Here is the golden close of love,
All my wooing is done.
Oh, the woods and the meadows,
Woods where we hid from the wet,
Stiles where we stayed to be kind,
Meadows in which we met!

Light, so low in the vale
You flash and lighten afar,
For this is the golden morning of love,
And you are his morning star.
Flash, I am coming, I come,
By meadow and stile and wood,
Oh, lighten into my eyes and heart,
Into my heart and blood!

Heart, are you great enough
For a love that never tires?
O heart, are you great enough for love?
I have heard of thorns and briers,
Over the meadows and stiles,
Over the world to the end of it
Flash for a million miles.

'Now sleeps the crimson petal'

Now sleeps the crimson petal, now the white;
Nor waves the cypress in the palace walk;
Nor winks the gold fin in the porphyry font.
The fire-fly wakens; waken thou with me.

Now droops the milkwhite peacock like a ghost,
And like a ghost she glimmers on to me.

Now lies the Earth all Danaë to the stars,
And all thy heart lies open unto me.

Now slides the silent meteor on, and leaves
A shining furrow, as thy thoughts in me.

Now folds the lily all her sweetness up,
And slips into the bosom of the lake.
So fold thyself, my dearest, thou, and slip
Into my bosom and be lost in me.

from **In Memoriam A.H.H.**

VII

Dark house, by which once more I stand
  Here in the long unlovely street,
Doors, where my heart was used to beat
  So quickly, waiting for a hand,

A hand that can be clasped no more–
  Behold me, for I cannot sleep,
And like a guilty thing I creep
  At earliest morning to the door.

He is not here; but far away
  The noise of life begins again,
And ghastly thro' the drizzling rain
  On the bald street breaks the blank day.

from **Maud**

I have led her home, my love, my only friend.
There is none like her, none.
And never yet so warmly ran my blood
And sweetly, on and on
Calming itself to the long-wished-for end,
Full to the banks, close on the promised good.

None like her, none,
Just now the dry-tongued laurels' pattering talk
Seemed her light foot along the garden walk,
And shook my heart to think she comes once more.
But even then I heard her close the door;
The gates of heaven are closed, and she is gone.

W. M. THACKERAY (1811–1863)

The Sorrows of Werther

Werther had a love for Charlotte
    Such as words could never utter;
Would you know how first he met her?
    She was cutting bread and butter.

Charlotte was a married lady,
    And a moral man was Werther,
And for all the wealth of Indies,
    Would do nothing for to hurt her.

So he sighed and pined and ogled.
    And his passion boiled and bubbled,
Till he blew his silly brains out,
    And no more by it was troubled.

Charlotte, having seen his body
    Borne before her on a shutter,
Like a well-conducted person,
    Went on cutting bread and butter.

HERBERT TRENCH (1865–1923)

She Comes Not

She comes not when Noon is on the roses–
Too bright is Day.
She comes not to the Soul till it reposes
From work and play.

But when Night is on the hills, and the great Voices
Roll in from Sea,
By starlight and candle-light and dreamlight
She comes to me.

WALT WHITMAN (1819–1892)

To a Stranger

Passing stranger! you do not know
How longingly I look upon you,
You must be he I was seeking,
Or she I was seeking
(It comes to me as a dream)

I have somewhere surely
Lived a life of joy with you,
All is recalled as we flit by each other,
Fluid, affectionate, chaste, matured,

You grew up with me,
Were a boy with me or a girl with me,
I ate with you and slept with you, your body has
    become
not yours only nor left my body mine only,

You give me the pleasure of your eyes,
face, flesh as we pass,
You take of my beard, breast, hands,
in return,

I am not to speak to you, I am to think of you
when I sit alone or wake at night, alone
I am to wait, I do not doubt I am to meet you again
I am to see to it that I do not lose you.

OSCAR WILDE (1856–1900)

from **The Ballad of Reading Gaol**

Yet each man kills the thing he loves,
    By each let this be heard,
Some do it with a bitter look,
    Some with a flattering word.
The coward does it with a kiss,
    The brave man with a sword!

Some kill their love when they are young,
    And some when they are old;
Some strangle with the hands of Lust,
    Some with the hands of Gold:
The kindest use a knife, because
    The dead so soon grow cold.

Some love too little, some too long,
    Some sell, and others buy;
Some do the deed with many tears,
    And some without a sigh:
For each man kills the thing he loves,
    Yet each man does not die.

To My Wife

With a copy of my poems

I can write no stately poem
   As a prelude to my lay;
From a poet to a poem
   I would dare to say.

For if of these fallen petals
   One to you seem fair,
Love will waft it till it settles
   On your hair.

And when wind and winter harden
   All the loveless land,
It will whisper of the garden,
   You will understand.

Love Song

Though the wind shakes lintel and rafter,
  And the priest sits mourning alone,
For the ruin that comes hereafter
  When the world shall be overthrown,
What matter the wind and weather
  To those that live for a day?
When my Love and I are together
  What matter what men may say?

I and my love where the wild red rose is,
  When hands grow weary and eyes are bright,
Kisses are sweet as the evening closes,
  Lips are reddest before the night,
And what matter if Death be an endless slumber
  And thorns the commonest crown for the head,
What matter if sorrow like wild weeds cumber,
  When kisses are sweetest, and lips are red?

I that am only the idlest singer
  That ever sang by a desolate sea,
A goodlier gift than song can bring her,

Sweeter than sound of minstrelsy,
For singers grow weary, and lips will tire,
 And winds will scatter the pipe and reed,
And even the sound of the silver lyre
 Sickens my heart in the days of need,
But never at all do I fail or falter
 For I know that Love is a god, and fair,
And if death and derision follow after,
 The only god worth a sin and a prayer.

And She and I are Queen and Master,
 Why should we care if a people groan
'Neath a despot's feet, or some red disaster
 Shatter the fool on his barren throne?
What matter if prisons and palaces crumble,
 And the red flag floats in the piled-up street,
When over the sound of the cannon's rumble
 The voice of my Lady is clear and sweet?
For the worlds are many and we are single,
 And sweeter to me when my Lady sings,
Than the cry when the East and the West world
    mingle,
 For clamour of battle, and the fall of Kings.

So out of the reach of tears and sorrow
  Under the wild-rose let us play,
And if death and severing come tomorrow,
  I have your kisses, sweet heart, today.

Magdalen College, Oxford

HUGO WILLIAMS (born 1942)

Siren Song

I phone from time to time, to see if she's
changed the music on her answerphone.
'Tell me in two words,' goes the recording,
'what you were going to tell in a thousand.'

I peer into that thought, like peering out
to sea at night, hearing the sound of waves
breaking on rocks, knowing she is there,
listening, waiting for me to speak.

Once in a while she'll pick up the phone
and her voice sings to me out of the past.
The hair on the back of my neck stands up
as I catch her smell for a second.

JOHN WILMOT, EARL OF ROCHESTER
(1647–1680)

Love and Life

All my past life is mine no more,
    The flying hours are gone,
Like transitory dreams given o'er,
Whose images are kept in store
    By memory alone.

The time that is to come is not;
    How can it then be mine?
The present moment's all my lot;
And that, as fast as it is got,
    Phillis, is only thine.

Then talk not of inconstancy,
    False hearts, and broken vows;
If I, by miracle, can be
This live-long minute true to thee,
    'Tis all that Heaven allows.

Ancient Person

Ancient Person, for whom I
All the flattering youth defy,
Long be it e'er thou grow old,
Aching, shaking, crazy cold;
But still continue as thou art,
Ancient Person of my heart.

On thy withered lips and dry,
Which like barren furrows lie,
Brooding kisses I will pour,
Shall thy youthful heart restore,
Such kind show'rs in autumn fall,
And a second spring recall;
Nor from thee will ever part,
Ancient Person of my heart.

Thy nobler parts, which but to name
In our sex would be counted shame,
By ages frozen grasp possessed
From their ice shall be released,
And, soothed by my reviving hand,

In former warmth and vigour stand.
All a lover's wish can reach,
For thy joy my love shall teach;
And for thy pleasure shall improve
All that art can add to love.
Yet still I love thee without art,
Ancient Person of my heart.

WILLIAM WORDSWORTH (1770–1850)

Sonnet

Surprised by joy – impatient as the wind
I turned to share the transport – Oh! with whom
But thee, deep buried in the silent tomb,
That spot which no vicissitude can find?
Love, faithful love, recalled thee to my mind –
But how could I forget thee? Though what power,
Even for the least division of an hour,
Have I been so beguiled as to be blind
To my most grievous loss! – That thought's return
Was the worst pang that sorrow ever bore,
Save one, one only, when I stood forlorn,
Knowing my heart's best treasure was no more;
That neither present time, nor years unborn
Could to my sight that heavenly face restore.

HUMBERT WOLFE (1885–1940)

The Lovers

I am the fiddler. Ere the world began
I had two notes, and only two. The one
with tumbled sunflakes dripping, I called man,
the second had no name and needed none.
I am the fiddler. I ike a golden fan
I folded the long feathers I had spun,
and, as I folded them, a shadow ran,
silver, between the music and the sun.
I threw my bow over the stars, and no man
remembered Krishna, but, till the world is done,
there are but these two notes, a single tune –
man, that I named before the world, and woman.
so named when she redeemed the fallen sun
with the vicarious silver of the moon.

The Thought

I will not write a poem for you,
because a poem, even the loveliest,
can only do what words can do –
stir the air, and dwindle, and be at rest.

Nor will I hold you with my hands, because
the bones of my hands on yours would press,
and you'd say after; 'Mortal was,
and crumbling, that lover's tenderness.'

But, I will hold you in a thought without moving
spirit or desire of will –
for I know no other way of loving,
that endures when the heart is still.

Things lovelier

You cannot dream
things lovelier
than the first love
I had of her.

Nor air is any
as magic shaken
as her breath in
the first kiss taken.

And who, in dreaming,
understands
her hands stretched like
a blind man's hands?

Open, trembling,
wise they were –
You cannot dream
things lovelier.

LADY MARY WROTH (c.1587–c.1652)

'The sun hath no long journey'

The sun hath no long journey now to go,
   While I a progress have in my desires;
   Disasters dead-low-water-like do show
   The sand, that overlooked my hoped-for hires.

Thus I remain like one that's laid in briars,
   Where turning brings new pain and certain woe,
   Like one, once burned, bids me avoid the fires,
   But love, true fire, will not let me be slow.

Obedience, fear and love do all conspire
   A worthless conquest gained to ruin me,
   Who did but feel the height of blest desire
   When danger, doubt and loss I straight did see.
Restless I live, consulting what to do,
And more I study, more I still undo.

'My thoughts thou hast supported'

My thoughts thou hast supported without rest,
My tired body here hath lain oppressed
With love and fear; yet be thou ever blessed;
Spring, prosper, last; I am alone unblest.

SIR THOMAS WYATT (1503–1542)

'They flee from me'

They flee from me that sometime did me seek
With naked foot, stalking in my chamber.
I have seen them gentle, tame, and meek,
That now are wild and do not remember
That sometime they put themself in danger
To take bread at my hand; and now they range,
Busily seeking with a continual change.

Thanked be fortune it hath been otherwise
Twenty times better; but once in special,
In thin array after a pleasant guise,
When her loose gown from her shoulders did fall,
And she me caught in her arms long and small;
Therewithal sweetly did me kiss
And softly said, 'Dear heart, how like you this?'

It was no dream: I lay broad waking.
But all is turned thorough my gentleness
Into a strange fashion of forsaking;

And I have leave to go of her goodness,
And she also, to use newfangleness.
But since that I so kindly am served
I would fain know what she hath deserved.

'I find no peace, and all my war is done'

I find no peace, and all my war is done:
I fear, and hope; I burn, and freeze like ice;
I fly above the wind, yet can I not arise;
And nought I have, and all the world I seize on;
That locketh nor loseth holdeth me in prison,
And holdeth me not, yet can I 'scape nowise:
Nor letteth me live, nor die at my devise,
And yet of death it giveth me occasion.
Without eye I see, and without tongue I 'plain;
I desire to perish, and yet I ask health;
I love another, and thus I hate myself;
I feed me in sorrow, and laugh in all my pain.
Likewise displeaseth me both death and life,
And my delight is causer of this strife.

W. B. YEATS (1865–1939)

When you are old

When you are old and grey and full of sleep,
And nodding by the fire, take down this book,
And slowly read, and dream of the soft look
Your eyes had once, and of their shadows deep;

How many loved your moments of glad grace,
And loved your beauty with love false or true,
But one man loved the pilgrim soul in you,
And loved the sorrows of your changing face;

And bending down beside the glowing bars,
Murmur, a little sadly, how Love fled
And paced upon the mountains overhead
And hid his face amid a crowd of stars.

Down by the Salley Gardens

Down by the salley gardens my love and I did meet;
She passed the salley gardens with little snow-white
feet.
She bid me take love easy, as the leaves grow on the
tree;
But I, being young and foolish, with her would not
agree.

In a field by the river my love and I did stand,
And on my leaning shoulder she laid her snow-white
hand.
She bid me take life easy, as the grass grows on the
weirs;
But I was young and foolish, and now am full of tears.

ACKNOWLEDGMENTS

HarperCollins Publishers gratefully acknowledge permission given by the following people and organisations to reproduce copyright poems in this anthology. We have made every effort to contact all copyright holders, but if any have been missed, the copyright holder should please contact us at: Reference Department, HarperCollins Publishers, Westerhill Road, Bishopbriggs, Glasgow G64 2QT.

Fleur Adcock: 'Revision' © Fleur Adcock is reprinted by permission of the author.

W. H. Auden: 'Stop all the clocks' and 'Warm are the still' and 'lucky miles' are reprinted by permission of the publishers, Faber and Faber Ltd.

Sir John Betjeman: 'In a Bath Teashop' is reprinted by permission of John Murray Publishers Ltd.

Earle Birney: 'From the Hazel Bough' reprinted by permission of the executor of the Estate of Earle Birney.

Raymond Carver: 'Late Fragment' from All of Us: The Collected Poems of Raymond Carver, published by Harvill, © Tess Gallacher, is reprinted by permission of The Random House Group Ltd.

Wendy Cope: 'Bloody Men' is reprinted by permission of the publishers, Faber and Faber Ltd.

T. S. Eliot: 'La figlia che piange' is reprinted by permission of the publishers, Faber and Faber Ltd.

U. A. Fanthorpe: 'Going Under' is reprinted by permission of Peterloo Poets.

Robert Graves: 'She tells her love while half asleep' and

'A Slice of Wedding Cake' from Complete Poems (1997) are reprinted by permission of the publisher, Carcanet Press Ltd.

Ivor Gurney: 'My heart makes songs on lonely roads' is reprinted by permission of the publisher, Carcanet Press.

A. E. Housman: 'Because I liked you better', 'Oh When I was in love with you' and 'White in the moon the long road lies' are reprinted by permission of the Society of Authors as the Literary Representative of the Estate of A. E. Housman.

Philip Larkin: 'The little lives of earth and form' is reprinted by permission of the publishers, Faber and Faber Ltd.

T. E. Lawrence: The epigraph to Seven Pillars of Wisdom is reprinted by permission of the Seven Pillars of Wisdom Trust, c/o Messrs Tweedie and Prideaux.

C. S. Lewis: 'As The Ruin Falls' by C. S. Lewis © C. S. Lewis Pte. Ltd, reprinted by permission.

Liz Lochhead: 'Sundaysong' is reprinted by permission from Dreaming Frankenstein & Collected Poems 1967–1984, published by Polygon.

Norman MacCaig: 'Water Tap', from Collected Poems by Norman MacCaig, published by Chatto & Windus, is reprinted by permission of the Random House Group.

Roger McGough: 'Ten Milk Bottles' from Summer with Monica is reprinted by permission of PFD on behalf of Roger McGough © 1967, Roger McGough.

Sorley Maclean: 'Multitude of the Skies', from Poems to Eimhir, is reprinted by permission of the publisher, Carcanet Press.

Leo Marks: 'The Life That I Have', from Between Silk and Cyanide by Leo Marks, is reprinted by permission of HarperCollins Publishers.

Edna St Vincent Millay: 'Love is not all', from Collected Poems, HarperCollins, copyright © 1928, 1955, is reprinted by permission of Elizabeth Barnett, literary executor.

Adrian Mitchell: 'Celia Celia' from Heart on the Left: Poems 1953–1984, is reprinted by permission of PFD on behalf of Adrian Mitchell. Educational Health Warning! Adrian Mitchell asks that none of his poems are used in connection to any examinations whatsoever. © 1996, Adrian Mitchell.

Edwin Morgan: 'One Cigarette' is reprinted by permission of the publisher, Carcanet Press Ltd.

Edwin Muir: 'The Confirmation' is reprinted by permission of the publishers, Faber and Faber Ltd.

John Frederick Nims: 'Love Poem' is reprinted by permission of Louisiana state University Press from *The Powers of Heaven and Earth: New and Selected Poems,* by John Frederick Nims. Copyright © 2002 by Bonnie Larkin Nims, Frank McReynolds Nims, Sarah Hoyt Nims Martin, Emily Anne Nims.

Dorothy Parker: 'Theory' and 'Comment' are reprinted by permission of Polinger Ltd

Brian Patten: 'Into my mirror has walked' is reprinted by permission of the author.

Henry Reed: 'Judging Distances' from 'Lessons of the War' is reprinted by permission of the Estate of the late Henry Reed, c/o The Royal Literary Fund.

William Soutar: 'The Halted Moment', 'The Tryst' and 'Who are These Children?' are reprinted by permission of the Trustees of the National Library of Scotland.

Hugo Williams: 'Siren Song' is reprinted by permission of the publishers, Faber and Faber Ltd.

W. B. Yeats: 'When you are old and grey' and 'Down by the Salley Gardens' are reprinted by permission of A. P. Watt Ltd on behalf of Michael B. Yeats.

INDEX OF TITLES

INDEX OF FIRST LINES